MORNING & EVENING DEVOTIONAL

LARGE PRINT WORD SEARCH

CHARLES H. SPURGEON

WHITAKER
HOUSE

Publisher's note:
This book contains word searches based on selected readings from Charles Spurgeon's *Morning and Evening*. Spurgeon's original text has been lightly edited for the modern reader. Words, expressions, and sentence structure have been updated for clarity and readability, while retaining the entirety of Spurgeon's original writings.

All Scripture quotations are taken from the King James Version (KJV) of the Holy Bible.

Morning And Evening Devotional Large Print Word Search
100 Puzzles from the Timeless Christian Classic

ISBN: 978-1-64123-912-7

Printed in Colombia

© 2022 by Whitaker House

Whitaker House
1030 Hunt Valley Circle
New Kensington, PA 15068
www.whitakerhouse.com

2 3 4 5 6 7 8 9 10 11 12 W 31 30 29 28 27 26 25 24 23

Morning

They did eat of the fruit of the land of Canaan that year.
—Joshua 5:12

Israel's weary wanderings were over, and the promised rest was attained. No more moving tents, fiery serpents, fierce Amalekites, and howling wildernesses. The Israelites came to the land that flowed with milk and honey, and they ate the old corn of the land. Perhaps this year, beloved Christian reader, this may be your case or mine. The prospect is joyful, and, if faith is actively exercised, it will yield pure delight. To be with Jesus in the rest that remains for the people of God is a cheering hope indeed, and to expect this glory so soon is a double bliss. Unbelief shudders at the Jordan, which still rolls between us and the good land, but let us rest assured that we have already experienced more ills than death at its worst can cause us. Let us banish every fearful thought and rejoice with exceeding great joy in the prospect that this year we will begin to *"ever be with the Lord"* (1 Thess. 4:17). Many will this year remain on earth to do service for their Lord. If this is our lot, there is no reason that the New Year's text should not still be true. *"We which have believed do enter into rest"* (Heb. 4:3). The Holy Spirit is the guarantee of our inheritance. He gives us "glory begun below." Those who are in heaven are secure; likewise, we on earth are kept safe in Christ Jesus. There, they triumph over their enemies; here, we have victories, too. Celestial spirits enjoy communion with their Lord; this privilege is not denied to us. They rest in His love; we have perfect peace in Him. They sing His praise; it is our privilege to bless Him, too. We will this year gather celestial fruits on earthly ground, where faith and hope have made the desert like the garden of the Lord. In the past, man ate angels' food; why not now? Oh, for grace to feed on Jesus and to eat of the fruit of the land of Canaan this year!

```
E  I  N  E  G  S  S  H  S  X  V  N  Z  I  H  P  Y  S  M  L
U  N  R  C  E  D  F  P  H  C  K  A  M  S  Z  M  R  L  I  R
H  D  C  E  L  E  S  T  I  A  L  A  Z  R  O  F  G  C  J  P
V  U  Q  D  Y  O  P  B  F  R  Q  S  E  A  O  D  Z  B  P  E
L  Q  E  X  M  X  K  Z  D  P  I  F  Y  E  K  P  S  F  E  A
I  N  H  E  R  I  T  A  N  C  E  T  R  L  R  R  K  B  U  C
T  H  O  Z  Z  U  O  W  S  M  T  A  S  I  E  I  B  L  F  E
P  O  X  K  U  D  U  C  A  X  X  B  U  T  J  V  U  I  Q  P
N  T  X  M  C  F  C  G  A  N  M  D  L  E  O  I  Q  S  P  U
I  L  U  E  K  D  R  H  P  W  D  G  X  S  I  L  F  S  U  P
T  F  U  N  B  E  L  I  E  F  G  E  A  K  C  E  J  Q  E  R
O  H  H  X  K  S  Y  D  B  E  O  H  R  R  E  G  V  Y  I  O
T  G  U  A  R  A  N  T  E  E  R  E  H  I  D  E  M  R  O  S
W  B  N  L  P  K  S  E  G  G  H  I  D  S  N  E  R  N  Q  P
X  W  Z  J  H  V  T  I  X  V  A  S  N  J  O  G  N  H  J  E
S  C  Q  O  O  C  Q  H  O  W  L  I  N  G  L  P  S  O  R  C
C  O  M  M  U  N  I  O  N  Q  X  M  V  K  F  G  Q  N  G  T
E  Y  T  R  I  U  M  P  H  O  Z  C  K  U  N  B  B  E  R  K
Y  B  T  R  L  Z  R  F  I  S  D  E  S  E  R  T  F  Y  Y  Z
G  E  C  O  T  A  M  A  L  E  K  I  T  E  S  Z  N  R  W  O
```

WANDERINGS	AMALEKITES	HOWLING	ISRAELITES
HONEY	PROSPECT	CHEERING	BLISS
UNBELIEF	REJOICE	GUARANTEE	INHERITANCE
TRIUMPH	CELESTIAL	SPIRITS	COMMUNION
PRIVILEGE	PEACE	DESERT	GARDEN

Evening

We will be glad and rejoice in thee.
—Song of Solomon 1:4

We will be glad and rejoice in thee." We will not open the gates of the year to the dolorous notes of the trombone, but to the sweet strains of the harp of joy and the grand sounds of the cymbals of gladness. *"O come, let us sing unto the LORD: let us make a joyful noise to the rock of our salvation"* (Ps. 95:1). We, the called and faithful and chosen, will drive away our griefs and set up our banners of confidence in the name of God. Let others lament over their troubles; we who have the sweetening tree to cast into Marah's bitter pool (see Exodus 15:23) will magnify the Lord with joy. Eternal Spirit, our precious Comforter, we, who are the temples in which You dwell, will never cease from adoring and blessing the name of Jesus. *"We will"*—we are resolved about it. Jesus must have the crown of our hearts' delight. We will not dishonor our Bridegroom by mourning in His presence. We are ordained to be the minstrels of the skies; let us rehearse our everlasting anthem before we sing it in the halls of the New Jerusalem. *"We will be glad and rejoice."* These words have one sense: double joy, blessing upon blessing. Does there need to be any limit to our rejoicing in the Lord? Do not men of grace find their Lord to be precious even now? What better fragrance do they have in heaven itself? *"We will be glad and rejoice in thee."* That last word is the meat in the dish, the kernel of the nut, the soul of the text. What blessings are laid up in Jesus! What rivers of infinite bliss have their source, yes, and every drop of their fullness, in Him! Since, O sweet Lord Jesus, You are the present portion of Your people, favor us this year with such a sense of Your preciousness that, from its first to its last day, we may be glad and rejoice in You. Let January open with joy in the Lord, and December close with gladness in Jesus.

```
V O T L R U S T R A I N S Y L O L Q Z K
W S L P N V Y W M L C N D I N V T E E E
E C S F G B V G D T R O M B O N E Y F R
S W Y W A F T H R A I B M U O U B U E N
S Q A M E N D L A M E N T G G L L H Y E
C E Z W B E C H X O K K W P G Y E J J L
X O W D M A T K A M Y L M L L J S O F S
E A F R W O L E C R B L E F A O S H G J
O R B Z Y Q B S N P P U V E D A I D W T
M I N S T R E L S I H U L Q N X N A A S
C O M F O R T E R W N P R N E R G B V E
T Q L J Q F E X K Y G G D O S Y X E D Y
V M F V N F T H F P Q M D T S M T X O C
M H J E R U S A L E M F E E W A C Z L B
F I U E X I T Y O L I R K S C G P C O I
K J E S U S M M N I W O E V B N L B R H
Y T E K A B A N N E R S B P T I V Y O Q
Q E P R E C I O U S N E S S D F E Y U F
C H O S E N B J M A V H Y T Q Y N C S E
W V B Q C D U C O N F I D E N C E V W A
```

DOLOROUS	NOTES	TROMBONE	STRAINS
HARP	CYMBALS	GLADNESS	CHOSEN
BANNERS	CONFIDENCE	LAMENT	SWEETENING
MAGNIFY	COMFORTER	MINSTRELS	JERUSALEM
BLESSING	KERNEL	JESUS	PRECIOUSNESS

Morning

I…will be their God.
—Jeremiah 31:33

Christian, here in this promise is all you need. In order to be happy, you need something that will satisfy you; is this not enough? If you can pour this promise into your cup, will you not say with David, "My cup runs over. (See Psalm 23:5.) I have more than my heart could wish for"? When His promise to be your God is fulfilled, are you not a possessor of all things? Desire is as insatiable as death, but He who fills *"all in all"* (Eph. 1:23) can fill it. Who can measure the capacity of our wishes? But the immeasurable wealth of God can more than overflow it. I ask you if you are not complete when God is yours? Do you need anything but God? Is not His all-sufficiency enough to satisfy you, if all else should fail? But you need more than quiet satisfaction; you desire rapturous delight. Come, soul; here is music fit for heaven in this your portion, for God is the Maker of heaven. Not all the music played by sweet instruments or drawn from strings can yield such melody as this sweet promise, *"I…will be their God."* Here is a deep sea of bliss, a shoreless ocean of delight. Come and bathe your spirit in it. Swim for an age, and you will find no shore; dive throughout eternity, and you will find no bottom. *"I… will be their God."* If this does not make your eyes sparkle and your heart beat high with bliss, then assuredly your soul is not in a healthy state. But you need more than present delights—you crave something concerning which you may exercise hope. What more can you hope for than the fulfillment of this great promise, *"I…will be their God"*? This is the masterpiece of all the promises. Its enjoyment makes a heaven below and will make a heaven above. Dwell in the light of your Lord, and let your soul always be ravished with His love. Extract all the *"marrow and fatness"* (Ps. 63:5) that this portion yields to you. Live up to your privileges, and rejoice with unspeakable joy.

```
H E D E S I R E H P D M P L X I T F X S
F P L P N D J W Q T E R O J R W I S H E
V U W T S Q L F P Y A F S L X S E S E B
N O N Q P E I G V R T J S E H I R O J Z
T H U A D P M D Z W H T E Z K N F R S D
K U A E C L M C O S I J S H U S U A O H
C X H P O U E T W S T G S D F A L P N P
H S C Q P V A J E I V B O C X T F T C S
R F A O C Y S B A B Y Z R X X I I U B A
I U P N P L U D L Y P W D H Z A L R Y L
S F A U O G R J T W Q X V C T B L O Z M
T W C Q P B A P H F M H O D L L E U C H
I P I H G R B K V T H P T R Q E D S C G
A O T B E V L A B S H O R E L E S S W T
N X Y U P A E O R K N Z H F W G G C S X
M W H W F O R X G M E A S U R E E I Q P
Z R I J L Y U T G P V A E B S D Y X O C
A Y H D U V W R M T P D N Y N K Q E H U
S U F F I C I E N C Y Z F U C R K O M P
C A Y P R O M I S E D H L S T K L I Q W
```

CHRISTIAN	PROMISE	HAPPY	POUR
SUFFICIENCY	CUP	PSALM	HEART
WISH	FULFILLED	POSSESSOR	DESIRE
INSATIABLE	DEATH	MEASURE	CAPACITY
IMMEASURABLE	WEALTH	SHORELESS	RAPTUROUS

Evening

Serve the LORD with gladness.
—Psalm 100:2

Delight in divine service is a token of acceptance. Those who serve God with a sad countenance, because they do what is unpleasant to them, are not serving Him at all; they bring the form of homage, but the life is absent. Our God requires no slaves to grace His throne. He is the Lord of the empire of love, and He would have His servants dressed in the uniform of joy. The angels of God serve Him with songs, not with groans. A murmur or a sigh would be mutiny in their ranks. Obedience that is not voluntary is disobedience, for the Lord looks at the heart, and if He sees that we serve Him from force, and not because we love Him, He will reject our offering. Service coupled with cheerfulness is heart-service and, therefore, true. Take away joyful willingness from the Christian, and you have removed the test of his sincerity. If a man is driven to battle, he is no patriot; but he who marches into the fray with flashing eye and beaming face, singing, "It is sweet to die for one's country," proves himself to be sincere in his patriotism. Cheerfulness is the support of our strength; in the joy of the Lord we are strong. It acts as the remover of difficulties. It is to our service what oil is to the wheels of a railroad car. Without oil the axle soon grows hot, and accidents occur; if there is not a holy cheerfulness to oil our wheels, our spirits will be clogged with weariness. The man who is cheerful in his service to God proves that obedience is his element; he can sing,

Make me to walk in Your commands,
  'Tis a delightful road.

Reader, let me put this question to you: Do you *"serve the LORD with gladness"*? Let us show the people of the world, who think our religion is slavery, that to us it is a delight and a joy! Let our gladness proclaim that we serve a good Master.

```
T E E A R H P N J D M I D K H P K O P X
T C M V S X E Z M M H L W L C U R P V V
G L P I X K U M U U J I C U G Q S M P O
S S I W K D C A U J O N L D S H R U U L
L I R U L M N B T T F U O J M W O R N U
F G E W S D P S E Y I A V C M Z O M P N
L H K O C H L E W O S N E Q S E U U L T
A H O M A G E N A Q B V Y B L W N R E A
Q M H K K O B T B C J R S Z T U I X A R
E U W X X V B Z J C C B S Q T N F O S Y
O S K Q B T Q E N M L E N E C K O B A V
M D K E O B G U D D L A P E R Z R X N D
I T G R O A N S O I H E I T V V M P T S
K O W T I V N S R T E H H T A E I S Z L
W W S H O C N S B S P N Z H Z N D C Y A
D A R J W K A C U O M P C O U I C U E V
B G Z R R D E M O N U E T E N M C E U E
X U W B J Q K N D G F D I V I N E K D S
D E L I G H T L P O A O E F I O H F D A
F W I L L I N G N E S S N Q J V W L X G
```

DELIGHT	DIVINE	SERVICE	TOKEN
ACCEPTANCE	UNPLEASANT	HOMAGE	ABSENT
SLAVES	EMPIRE	LOVE	UNIFORM
SONG	GROANS	MURMUR	SIGH
MUTINY	OBEDIENCE	VOLUNTARY	WILLINGNESS

Morning

I will help thee, saith the Lord.
—Isaiah 41:14

Let us hear the Lord Jesus speak these words to each one of us: "I will help you. It is but a small thing for Me, your God, to help you. Consider what I have done already. What! not help you? Why, I bought you with My blood. What! not help you? I have died for you; and if I have done the greater, will I not do the lesser? Help you! It is the least thing I will ever do for you. I have done more and will do more. Before the world began, I chose you. I made the covenant for you. I laid aside My glory and became a man for you. I gave up My life for you, and if I did all of this, I will surely help you now! In helping you, I am giving you what I have bought for you already. If you had need of a thousand times as much help, I would give it to you. You require little compared with what I am ready to give. It is much for you to need, but it is nothing for me to bestow. Help you? Do not fear! If there were an ant at the door of your granary asking for help, it would not ruin you to give him a handful of your wheat; you are nothing but a tiny insect at the door of My all-sufficiency. I will help you." O my soul, is this not enough? Do you need more strength than the omnipotence of the united Trinity? Do you need more wisdom than exists in the Father, more love than displays itself in the Son, or more power than is manifest in the influences of the Spirit? Bring your empty pitcher here! Surely this well will fill it. Hurry, gather up your needs, and bring them here— your emptiness, your sorrows, your deficiencies. Behold, this river of God is full for your supply. What can you desire besides? Go forth, my soul, in this your might. The eternal God is your Helper!

Fear not, I am with thee;
    Oh, be not dismay'd!
For I am thy God;
    I will still give thee aid.

```
G C A O N Q C E H L Q Y D Q G V L H B Y
D Z W B S G O A M E I X Q O V T G J Q A
H M U N P A N E O S S M L B N U C U S K
C A S M N S S T N S N T E H U B L N C C
W N N R Q K I L W E B R W G U Y G O J L
G I Z D P H D V D R B I Y L M K R T R R
D F H W F G E X Q O T N O R K I E H K V
H E G H S U R J Q V Y I I T R C A I Z N
Q S Y L Y P L B D U K T O Q V F T N W O
P T L F O V V B Q O N Y M C J B E G O Z
L C I D J R L I P X A E N U K R R R R R
I I N D W M Y D T M M S I T L Q S X D N
P D S Y C F A T H E R S P M G Y P V S C
D K E H H V M I P T Q G O S U R E L Y R
S V C M S N G O D G V E T C U O A M H H
K M T R Y L Z I V C X L E H D A K A V L
H X S Y M A R S M A L L N D G O H L M Y
D A L R E A D Y P T K N C L X L C A F J
Z E F I R W I S D O M N E Z Y L S N Q X
D G R A N A R Y E G Z W R E Q U I R E W
```

SPEAK   WORDS   SMALL   GOD
CONSIDER   ALREADY   GREATER   LESSER
GLORY   SURELY   REQUIRE   NOTHING
GRANARY   HANDFUL   INSECT   OMNIPOTENCE
TRINITY   WISDOM   FATHER   MANIFEST

Evening

Messiah [shall] be cut off, but not for himself.
—Daniel 9:26

Blessed be His name, there was no cause of death in Him. Neither original nor actual sin had defiled Him; therefore, death had no claim on Him. No man could have taken His life from Him justly, for He had done no man wrong. No man could have even struck Him down by force unless He had been pleased to yield Himself to die. But one sins and another suffers. Justice was offended by us, but it found its satisfaction in Him. Rivers of tears, mountains of offerings, seas of the blood of bullocks, and hills of frankincense could not have accomplished the removal of sin. But Jesus was cut off for us, and the cause of wrath was cut off at once, for sin was put away forever. Herein is wisdom, whereby substitution, the sure and speedy way of atonement, was devised! Herein is condescension, which brought Messiah, the Prince, to wear a crown of thorns and to die on the cross! Herein is love, which led the Redeemer to lay down His life for His enemies! It is not enough, however, to admire the spectacle of the innocent bleeding for the guilty; we must make sure of our interest in it. The special purpose of the Messiah's death was the salvation of His church. Have we a part and a lot among those for whom He gave His life as a ransom? Did the Lord Jesus stand as our Representative? Are we healed by His stripes? It would be a terrible thing indeed if we would come short of a portion in His sacrifice; it would be better for us if we had never been born. Solemn as the question is, it is a joyful circumstance that it is one that may be answered clearly and without mistake. To all who believe on Him, the Lord Jesus is a present Savior, and upon them all the blood of reconciliation has been sprinkled. Let all who trust in the merit of Messiah's death be joyful at every remembrance of Him, and let their holy gratitude lead them to the fullest consecration to His cause.

```
Z Z P M D R N T S U Y M K S O M Y G Q P
A T O N E M E N T P P C Y Z D F K S Y T
B V S W K W L M R G E Q E D F O K R P P
U S C T Q Z O C O U H E Q N O P T Z G W
L W N O R B F L C V G P D G S A F X S R
L J S E N I A N M T A D M Y P P R G U O
O N J A Z D P K M N P L H A E X A G B N
C K P V L M E E P A W B D D C E N V S G
K P Z X F V G S S H M N P T T B K T T S
S O B Q D X A I C M E S S I A H I T I P
O R V Q Q T S T Y E B D J N C C N J T G
Z T R A A A A N I Y N B G P L T C B U O
Z I R A K C A J T O L S K B E B E V T T
Q O R X N J H Y V Q N Q I R G Z N V I G
C N X B L D C A T E A R S O R F S U O R
Y I E L D D O Z J Z B I K K N Z E U N D
R B T V W T A M Q R E D E E M E R T E X
O D E F I L E D X F L O E R P M S I Z W
W J O R I G I N A L Q J U S T L Y I V X
C P U C E M J B B P B E N I L P X Q R N
```

ORIGINAL	DEFILED	JUSTLY	WRONG
YIELD	TEARS	BULLOCKS	FRANKINCENSE
REMOVAL	SUBSTITUTION	SPEEDY	ATONEMENT
CONDESCENSION	MESSIAH	REDEEMER	SPECTACLE
SALVATION	RANDOM	STRIPES	PORTION

Morning

Abel was a keeper of sheep.
—Genesis 4:2

As a shepherd, Abel sanctified his work to the glory of God and offered a sacrifice of blood on his altar. The Lord respected Abel and his offering. This early type of Christ is exceedingly clear and distinct. Like the first streak of light that tinges the East at sunrise, it does not reveal everything, but it clearly manifests the great fact that the sun is coming. As we see Abel, a shepherd and yet a priest, offering a sweet-smelling sacrifice unto God, we discern our Lord, who brings before His Father a sacrifice to which Jehovah ever has respect. Abel was hated by his brother—hated without a cause; even so was the Savior. The natural and carnal man hated the accepted man, in whom the Spirit of grace was found, and did not rest until his blood had been shed. Abel fell and sprinkled his altar and sacrifice with his own blood; therein sets forth the Lord Jesus slain by the enmity of man, while serving as a Priest before the Lord. *"The good shepherd giveth his life for the sheep"* (John 10:11). Let us weep over Him as we view Him slain by the hatred of mankind, staining the horns of His altar with His own blood. Abel's blood speaks. The Lord said to Cain, *"The voice of thy brother's blood crieth unto me from the ground"* (Gen. 4:10). The blood of Jesus has a mighty tongue, and the import of its prevailing cry is not vengeance, but mercy. It is precious beyond all preciousness to stand at the altar of our Good Shepherd—to see Him bleeding there as the slaughtered Priest, and then to hear His blood speaking peace to all His flock, peace in our consciences, peace between Jew and Gentile, peace between man and his offended Maker, peace down all the ages of eternity for blood-washed men. Abel was the first shepherd in order of time, but our hearts will ever place Jesus first in order of excellence. Great Keeper of the sheep, we the people of Your pasture bless You with our whole hearts when we see You slain for us.

```
Q B A B E L C E H B E O M R R U N V Y F
T W X D C L Q R E H Y U B E F W A T H H
G Y A L F T U K N P T T B S W N T V E D
A T M D R P Q J M V M U X P T R U E D L
P Q U S E J Q E I S N F H E L B R N Q V
A R S Y H T X X T U C W T C X L A G G I
N C E A A V G U Y N Y N I T S O L E P N
M H S V C K I W K R G V I E X O O A R E
V U H B A R F I U I J A Q D R D S N I N
B Y I J E I I Z P S Q O V E Q N Y C E W
L D C W J U L F F E X N F L P C L E S E
I I K A W C O I I K L V D F A H A F T O
M E R Q R J X F N C D V S Z E O P I T A
R F K F B N Z H V G E T H G R R D C N L
W B F J G B A W R K U P Q N K N I S J T
B R X H R T W L Y K Z D D D S S P N Q A
D M G Q A Q E F P G W W E E P D J N G R
R Y Q L C E S J Z G G W O R L N A Q J
E A F O E C D S A N C T I F I E D I N Z
R S T R E A K X G G S P R I N K L E D T
```

ABEL	SANCTIFIED	SACRIFICE	BLOOD
ALTAR	RESPECTED	OFFERING	STREAK
SUNRISE	NATURAL	CARNAL	GRACE
SPRINKLED	ENMITY	PRIEST	WEEP
HORNS	CAIN	PREVAILING	VENGEANCE

Evening

Turn away mine eyes from beholding vanity;
and quicken thou me in thy way.
—Psalm 119:37

There are various kinds of vanity. The cap and bells of the fool, the mirth of the world, the dance, the lyre, and the cup of the indulgent—all these things men know to be vanities. They display their proper name and title prominently. Far more treacherous are those equally conceited things, *"the cares of this world, and the deceitfulness of riches"* (Mark 4:19). A person may follow vanity as much in his business as an actor seeks it in the theater. If he is spending his life in amassing wealth, he passes his days in a vain show. Unless we follow Christ and make God the great purpose of our lives, we differ only in appearance from the most frivolous. It is clear that there is much need of the first prayer of our text, *"Turn away mine eyes from beholding vanity."* In the second prayer, *"Quicken thou me in thy way,"* the psalmist confessed that he was dull, heavy, lethargic, all but dead. Perhaps, dear reader, you feel the same. We are so sluggish that the best motives cannot quicken us, apart from the Lord Himself. What! Will not hell quicken me? Will I think of sinners perishing, and yet not be awakened? Will not heaven quicken me? Can I think of the reward that awaits the righteous and yet be cold? Will not death quicken me? Can I think of dying and standing before my God yet be slothful in my Master's service? Will not Christ's love constrain me? Can I think of His dear wounds, can I sit at the foot of His cross and not be stirred with fervency and zeal? It seems so! No mere consideration can quicken us to zeal, but God Himself must do it; hence, the cry, *"Quicken **thou** me"* (emphasis added). The psalmist breathed out his whole soul in vehement pleadings; his body and his soul united in prayer. *"Turn away mine eyes,"* says the body. *"Quicken thou me,"* cries the soul. This is an appropriate prayer for every day. O Lord, hear it in my case this night.

```
R P M L P A C B T K B E H O L D I N G B
N M Z C C J D O E T G H T C R N F P J M
E E B L V O Y Z R L Y M U H S R O R B E
P R A F A R N G J P L P M F U T O O I O
U T T G A C X C L M M S N R J P L M N Q
H S P H Y M T H E G F M H I H Q N I D L
H D Z S E Y V O P I S Y N V R X Y N U R
G Q K Z A A C C R J T A Z O S L Z E L Y
R M U R B L T Z W C P E N L N X M N G O
V A N I T Y M E G T U R D O V U M T E P
X I K T I I R I R D P V J U C N E L N V
O T P B M T E L S B R Q R S H A Y Y T L
W D D L I C M C T T S T I J W V Y W S
L U A Z R L E T H A R G I C C V M G N O
O D F Q T K S K Z L W T X V K H E R M U
L K Q C M J Q Y R H Z E A L E I N C
E Q U A L L Y C I R S Z O H N V L S E U
O W U I U R E P U E T J L P R O P E R H
V Q Z H S D E C E I T F U L N E S S E L
U J A M A S S I N G J U T Q L T L V S J
```

VANITY	BELLS	FOOL	MIRTH
LYRE	INDULGENT	PROPER	PROMINENTLY
EQUALLY	CONCEITED	DECEITFULNESS	RICHES
ACTOR	THEATER	AMASSING	FRIVOLOUS
BEHOLDING	PSALMIST	LETHARGIC	ZEAL

Morning

Your heavenly Father.
—Matthew 6:26

God's people are doubly His children: they are His by creation and by adoption in Christ. Hence they are privileged to call Him, *"Our Father which art in heaven"* (Luke 11:2). *Father*—oh, what a precious word that is! Here is authority: *"If then I be a father, where is mine honour?"* (Mal. 1:6). Here is affection mingled with authority. This kind of authority does not provoke rebellion. If you are children, where is your obedience? This kind of required obedience is most cheerfully given: it would not be withheld even if it could be. The obedience that God's children yield to Him must be loving obedience. Do not approach the service of God as slaves do their taskmaster's toil, but follow His commands, because that is your Father's way. Yield your bodies *"as instruments of righteousness"* (Rom. 6:13), because righteousness is your Father's will, and His will should be the will of His child. Father!—here is a kingly attribute so sweetly veiled in love that the King's crown is forgotten in the King's face, and His scepter becomes not a rod of iron, but a silver scepter of mercy; the scepter indeed seems to be forgotten in the tender hand of Him who wields it. Father!—here is honor and love. How great is a father's love for his children! What friendship cannot do and mere benevolence will not attempt, a father's heart and hand must do for his children. They are his offspring, and he must bless them; they are his children, and he must show himself strong in their defense. If an earthly father watches over his children with unceasing love and care, how much more does our heavenly Father? "Abba, Father!" He who can say this, has uttered better music than cherubim or seraphim can reach. There is heaven in the depth of that word—*Father!* There is all I can ask, all my necessities can demand, and all my wishes can desire. I have all in all now and throughout eternity when I can say, "Father."

```
Y G A I T H I G W M I N G L E D N X Q C
W K Q K E E L P R O V O K E Z S U F T R
D I B V A N X Z K A R A K O G C B V U E
B I T W L C H E Q M M M C V P E N I N A
I B N H Z E W W A I N Q T Z L P G U N T
W F R S H Y T V F D Z C O B M T R R M I
G X J R T E T Q G Q X H I T A E B K B O
Y I Q E V R L T I D N I L G L R V Z Q N
I G V S N E U D A M C L V V L X S C Z R
L G O E G K P M O Q V D M Q Y S A H U E
S S F R N E V A E S Q R H P D R U E S B
G Q N R H K N G U N X E E R V H T E R E
A T T R I B U T E J T N R E B J H R M L
E P W D O U B L Y T X S K C Z P O F L L
Z V G R A F F E C T I O N I F B R U B I
R W L L O V I N G X K H Q O D X I L V O
K I N G L Y C K K G F T V U I Y T L H N
I G J T I U Y C I Y H U S S R M Y Y B U
J K Q Q N V R Y O X M B B L L K M R M K
W M H P U Y H L V P F C H E A V E N K R
```

DOUBLY	CHILDREN	CREATION	HENCE
HEAVEN	PRECIOUS	AUTHORITY	AFFECTION
MINGLED	PROVOKE	REBELLION	CHEERFULLY
GIVEN	WITHHELD	LOVING	TOIL
INSTRUMENTS	KINGLY	ATTRIBUTE	SCEPTER

DAY 5

Evening

All they that heard it wondered at those things.
—Luke 2:18

We must not cease to wonder at the great marvels of our God. It would be very difficult to draw a line between holy wonder and real worship, for when the soul is overwhelmed with the majesty of God's glory, though it may not express itself in song or even utter its voice with bowed head in humble prayer, yet it silently adores. Our incarnate God is to be worshipped as "the Wonderful." That God should consider His fallen creature, man, and, instead of sweeping him away with the *"besom [broom] of destruction"* (Isa. 14:23), should Himself undertake to be man's Redeemer and to pay his ransom price, is, indeed, marvelous! But to each believer redemption is most marvelous as he views it in relation to himself. It is a miracle of grace, indeed, that Jesus would forsake the thrones and royalties above to suffer a shameful death below *for you.* Let your soul lose itself in wonder, for wonder is, in this way, a very practical emotion. Holy wonder will lead you to grateful worship and heartfelt thanksgiving. It will cause within you godly watchfulness. You will be afraid to sin against such a love as this. Feeling the presence of the mighty God in the gift of His dear Son, you will *"put off thy shoes from off thy feet, for the place whereon thou standest is holy ground"* (Exod. 3:5). You will be moved at the same time to glorious hope. If Jesus has done such marvelous things on your behalf, you will feel that heaven itself is not too great for your expectation. Who can be astonished at anything, when he has once been astonished at the manger and the Cross? What is left that is wonderful after one has seen the Savior? Dear reader, it may be that, from the quietness and solitude of your life, you are scarcely able to imitate the shepherds of Bethlehem, who told what they had seen and heard, but you can, at least, fill up the circle of the worshippers before the throne by wondering at what God has done.

```
S W Z P O K Y J O V E R W H E L M E D J
W O O H F V L R T R E P K Y L U H F O J
R X U N Z G A P A J P K J C J B T U N O
B N M L D S D A S N C C B L A G L X D A
B M Z S N E O N I T S F E H T N B N I P
Y Q A J Z K R G L A B O F E J Z Q F F B
G Y S R C S D P E P O X M E S Q Y W F T
K U H Z V J D A N X T X S Z W B S O I B
E K D U T E F C T D S D R K E I K R C L
X K K M M H L R L L Z C V Q E Z Q S U O
P I U U L B D S Y Y N L T P P O M H L Z
R M L V E E L T Y I X O B M I K F I T W
E U M I S H P E W B H O L Y N V P P G I
S I O F V R T B E D W D K K G B B E P X
S V M A R V E L O U S J C F I E B K R J
J P P W S W I N C A R N A T E N I G A T
S W P Y W V J B Y W M A D O R E S T Y R
P Y V F M P B O W E D D J S K P Q P E L
M Y B B D I K Q F O R S A K E I Y F R U
O W U N D E R T A K E M A J E S T Y W K
```

WONDER	MARVELS	DIFFICULT	HOLY
WORSHIP	SOUL	OVERWHELMED	MAJESTY
EXPRESS	BOWED	HUMBLE	PRAYER
SILENTLY	ADORES	INCARNATE	SWEEPING
UNDERTAKE	RANSOM	MARVELOUS	FORSAKE

Morning

Therefore, brethren, we are debtors.
—Romans 8:12

As God's creatures, we are all debtors to Him: to obey Him with all our bodies, souls, and strength. Having broken His commandments, as we all have, we are debtors to His justice, and we owe to Him a vast amount that we are not able to pay. But, of the Christian, it can be said that he does not owe God's justice anything, for Christ has paid the debt His people owed. For this reason, the believer owes even more to love. I am a debtor to God's grace and forgiving mercy; but I am no debtor to His justice, for He will never accuse me of a debt that has already been paid. Christ said, *"It is finished"* (John 19:30), and by that He meant that whatever His people owed was wiped away forever from the book of remembrance. Christ, to the uttermost, has satisfied divine justice. The account is settled. The handwriting is nailed to the cross. The receipt is given, and we are debtors to God's justice no longer. But then, because we are not debtors to our Lord in that sense, we become debtors to God ten times more than we would have been otherwise. Christian, pause and ponder for a moment. What a debtor you are to divine sovereignty! How much you owe to His unbiased love, for He gave His own Son that He might die for you. Consider how much you owe to His forgiving grace that, after ten thousand affronts, He loves you as infinitely as ever. Consider what you owe to His power: how He has raised you from your death in sin; how He has preserved your spiritual life; how He has kept you from falling; and how, though a thousand enemies have beset your path, you have been able to continue on your way. Consider what you owe to His immutability: though you have changed a thousand times, He has not changed once. You are as deep in debt as you can be to every attribute of God. To God you owe yourself, and all you have. Yield yourself as a *"living sacrifice"*; it is but your *"reasonable service"* (Rom. 12:1).

```
G U T X V X M S N P K L N V V P H D T Z
N H B I E X M A Q A Z N N O X R H G F N
D U N B I A S E D K I W V Y S E T R G T
W F O R G I V I N G Y L I A T S J L V G
S W K F D A R Y Y U J E C R E I Y H I
I N F I N I T E L Y P X P D E R M Q K O
G O G F Q Z Y Z N D S O H B N V M R Z T
Z Y C A D E Z F C B E H Z I G E U E C O
X D G F Q J U Q Y C P B D R T D T M R J
L E I O H J H N C T W R T R H A A E E Q
K L M E R C Y C M L I Y D O R K B M A C
I A H O O Y E K S E H F P Q R N I B T W
M V N P J U S T I C E T B P R S L R U R
B I Y O O P O D F P O N D E R J I A R P
H A N D W R I T I N G A Q O D Z T N E H
Z N P Q T H O U S A N D F I R O Y C S Z
K E R E C E I P T O W X E W A E C E B E
C O M M A N D M E N T S N Z H U R Y A V
I R J G H W C S O V E R E I G N T Y C F
U T T E R M O S T E D A F F R O N T S S
```

CREATURES	DEBTORS	STRENGTH	COMMANDMENTS
MERCY	JUSTICE	REMEMBRANCE	UTTERMOST
HANDWRITING	NAILED	RECEIPT	PONDER
SOVEREIGNTY	UNBIASED	FORGIVING	THOUSAND
AFFRONTS	INFINITELY	PRESERVED	IMMUTABILITY

Evening

*Tell me…where thou feedest, where thou
makest thy flock to rest at noon.*
—Song of Solomon 1:7

These words express the desire of the believer to follow Christ and his longing for present communion with Him. Where do You feed Your flock? In Your house? I will go, if I may find You there. In private prayer? Then I will pray without ceasing. In the Word? Then I will read it diligently. In Your commandments? Then I will walk in them with all my heart. Tell me where You feed, for wherever You stand as the Shepherd, there will I lie down as a sheep; for none but You can supply my need. I cannot be satisfied to be apart from You. My soul hungers and thirsts for the refreshment of Your presence. "Where do You make Your flock to rest at noon?" For whether it is at dawn or at noon, my only rest must be where You are and Your beloved flock. My soul's rest must be a grace-given rest, and it can be found only in You. Where is the shadow of that rock? Why should I not repose underneath it? *"Why should I be as one that turneth aside by the flocks of thy companions?"* (Song 1:7). You have companions—why should I not be one? Satan tells me that I am unworthy, but I always was unworthy. Yet You have long loved me; therefore, my unworthiness cannot be a barrier to my having fellowship with You now. It is true I am weak in faith and prone to fall, but my very feebleness is the reason why I should always be where You feed Your flock, so that I may be strengthened and preserved in safety beside the still waters. Why should I turn away from You? There is no reason why I should, but there are a thousand reasons why I should not, for Jesus beckons me to come. If He withdrew Himself a little, it was only to make me prize His presence more. Now that I am grieved and distressed at being away from Him, He will lead me once again to that sheltered nook where the lambs of His fold are shielded from the burning sun.

```
Z O N B A C F E E B L E N E S S T X R Q
X Y S O R E F R E S H M E N T P C S T N
A U U Q V Z Q V A W B F G V A R J G G S
D I L I G E N T L Y J E S U S I R A D H
C D O W P R S G S I G Z G C B Z A Q F E
E V K U X M V U C B R U C Y U E S U L P
A G V U D T A G W Q I G F A C I A X O H
S K R O O J L A H O E H U K Y H T I C E
I B H T L D H H Z E V K I C J S I X K R
N B U N W O R T H Y E M H G O H S E L D
G W E E M J P W Q E D G H F I E F X R E
Y H A C Y R E P O S E G L J T E I P E Y
I D J L K U N D E R N E A T H P E R K F
J N K G O O N U B S N Z D U F H D I Q N
Y C Y C W M N O E E L D U X O Y A V S O
M F E L L O W S H I P O Y B E Q O A R O
B F F G Q R S H E L T E R E D T R T Z K
J R U Y J E Q F U A W J Q U L J R E M D
K I T Z U G M E L D M Z V T G G D A G Y
E I W Q O B J C O M P A N I O N S D E D
```

FLOCK	PRIVATE	CEASING	DILIGENTLY
SHEPHERD	SHEEP	SATISFIED	REFRESHMENT
REPOSE	UNDERNEATH	COMPANIONS	UNWORTHY
FELLOWSHIP	FEEBLENESS	JESUS	BECKONS
PRIZE	GRIEVED	SHELTERED	NOOK

Morning

David inquired of the Lord.
—2 Samuel 5:23

When David made this inquiry, he had just fought the Philistines and gained a signal victory. The Philistines had come up in great hosts, but, by the help of God, David had easily put them to flight. Note, however, that when they came a second time, David did not go up to fight them without inquiring of the Lord. Once he had been victorious, and he might have said, as many have in other cases, "I will be victorious again; I may rest quite sure that, if I have conquered once, I will triumph yet again. Why should I bother to seek the Lord's direction?" Not so, David. He had gained one battle by the strength of the Lord; he would not venture on another until he had ensured the same. He inquired, "Should I go up against them?" He waited until God's sign was given. Learn from David to take no step without God. Christian, if you would know the path of duty, take God for your compass; if you would steer your ship through the dark billows, put the tiller into the hand of the Almighty. Many rocks might be escaped, if we would let our Father take the helm; many shoals or quicksand we might well avoid, if we would leave to His sovereign will to choose and to command. The Puritan said, "As sure as ever a Christian carves for himself, he'll cut his own fingers"; this is a great truth. Said another old clergyman, "He who goes before the cloud of God's providence goes on a fool's errand"; and so he does. We must mark God's providence leading us; and if providence tarries, tarry until providence comes. He who goes before providence will be very glad to run back again. *I will instruct thee and teach thee in the way which thou shalt go* (Ps. 32:8) is God's promise to His people. Let us, then, take all our perplexities to Him, and say, "Lord, what would You have me to do?" Do not leave your room this morning without inquiring of the Lord.

```
U F D J L E M P S P O E N S U R E D D F
I T B C A D O Z V P Q A D Y F A D Y W B
N S C V R Y E N U Y L O A V Z P N E V I
S E L N E M N T S Y M L V C N C T T I L
V E E F S E C P L U L N I P S N Q A N L
U K R U T Z O S Z H K K D U T T U X Q O
C J G O N I N Q U I R I N G B M I L U W
C O Y E P J Q F N E D F D V J O C O I S
I Z M W A A U Q J F V P X C I V K A R Z
V D A V N D E P D C F W V V E R S V Y Z
D Q N C P D R S F U B A T T L E A X C A
J K E C R S E O Z L T H J L Z U N I O A
O Z K S L J D J K F W Y R S K Q D J V C
A X H O M P S T Z S D M N H V K D U I X
Z M L C F A B I A N K K Q O P Z J O C C
S H O S T S A L G G S S B A L J M A T S
I O A D P Z T L E N Q U B L Q Z S V O K
C G D L C Y Y E K O A D P S Y B O G R U
T F L I G H T R T M S L M B U Q J B Y G
Z N Y P H I L I S T I N E S P A T H F O
```

DAVID	INQUIRY	PHILISTINES	SIGNAL
VICTORY	HOSTS	FLIGHT	INQUIRING
REST	CONQUERED	SEEK	BATTLE
ENSURED	PATH	DUTY	BILLOWS
TILLER	SHOALS	QUICKSAND	CLERGYMAN

Evening

Lead us not into temptation;
but deliver us from evil [or, the evil one].
—Luke 11:4

What we are taught to seek or shun in prayer, we should equally pursue or avoid in action. Therefore, we should avoid temptation earnestly, seeking to walk guardedly in the path of obedience, so that we may never tempt the devil to tempt us. We are not to enter the thicket in search of the lion. Dearly might we pay for such presumption. A lion may cross our paths or leap on us from the thicket, but we have nothing to do with hunting it. He who meets with a lion, even though he wins the day, will find it a stern struggle. Let the Christian pray that he may be spared from the encounter. Our Savior, who experienced what temptation meant, thus earnestly admonished His disciples: *"Pray that ye enter not into temptation"* (Luke 22:40). But no matter what we do, we will be tempted; hence the prayer *"deliver us from evil."* God had one Son without sin; but He has no son without temptation. The natural *"man is born unto trouble, as the sparks fly upward,"* (Job 5:7), and the Christian man is born to temptation just as certainly. We must always be on watch against Satan, because, like a thief, he gives no warning of his approach. Believers who have had experience in the ways of Satan know that there are certain seasons when he will most probably make an attack, just as at certain seasons bleak winds may be expected. Thus the Christian is put on a double guard by fear of danger, and the danger is averted by preparing to meet it. Prevention is better than cure: it is better to be so well armed that the devil will not attack you than to endure the perils of the fight, even though you come off a conqueror. Pray this evening first that you may not be tempted, and next that if temptation is permitted, you may be delivered from the evil one.

```
T E M P T A T I O N Y W I K P B O H G N
R T J E B V S W J F K Y L D R L N U W Z
L H I K H X U Z I P Q Q Y F E E S N U U
G I A C W A T O N N B D T Z S A T T B N
O E O P E E G U U H D Z H H U K E I N I
G F J N Y S P A R E D S I E M N R N G K
X H Z Q S M J P Q V H B C H P N N G B S
L D G D V K Y K L U D G K Y T H O D I W
D M Z U A I P U L H E K E Y I C X H U T
P L D A A S A X E H E X T P O G Z X H A
Q W E O D R D E A R L Y V U N L K S Z P
G Y T A Y M D Q M M L U A W L I X T V I
C N M G P A O E S B N M G W H P H R B R
X M U Q E V L N D A J C V Q M S I U B N
L Y A A C O C L I L T M P A O I V G P S
E K P P T I E X U S Y A F I I F N G Q I
E Y Y I I D U Y E C H H N K Q T J L H O
N P I L D Q X C Y W L E Y S N P U E I Q
W A R N I N G T B W X F D B Q M E I W D
I C P O P U R S U E J O V W S H U N X I
```

SHUN	PURSUE	AVOID	TEMPTATION
GUARDEDLY	THICKET	LION	DEARLY
PRESUMPTION	LEAP	HUNTING	STERN
STRUGGLE	SPARED	ADMONISHED	SATAN
THIEF	WARNING	BLEAK	WINDS

Morning

And his allowance was a continual allowance given him of the king, a daily rate for every day, all the days of his life.
—2 Kings 25:30

Jehoiachin was not sent away from the king's palace with a store to last him for months, but his provision was given to him as a daily pension. Herein he well depicts the happy position of all the Lord's people. A daily portion is all that a person really needs. We do not need tomorrow's supplies; that day has not yet dawned, and its needs are as yet unborn. The thirst that we may suffer in the month of June does not need to be quenched in February, for we do not feel it yet. If we have enough for each day as the days arrive, we will never know need. Sufficient for the day is all that we can enjoy. We cannot eat, drink, or wear more than the day's supply of food and clothing. The surplus gives us the care of storing it and the anxiety of watching against a thief. One walking stick helps a traveler, but a bundle of sticks is a heavy burden. Enough is not only as good as a feast, but is all that the truest glutton can enjoy. This is all that we should expect; a craving for more than this is ingratitude. When our Father does not give us more, we should be content with our daily allowance. Jehoiachin's case is ours. We have a sure portion, a portion given to us by the King. It is a gracious and a perpetual portion. Here is surely ground for thankfulness. Beloved Christian, in matters of grace, you need a daily supply. You have no store of strength. Day by day, you must seek help from above. It is a very sweet assurance that a daily portion is provided for you. In the Word, through the ministry, by meditation, in prayer, and in waiting on God, you will receive renewed strength. In Jesus, all necessary things are laid up for you. Then enjoy your ongoing allowance. Never go hungry while the daily bread of grace is on the table of mercy.

```
T Y H X C E K A T L P Z C B G U D J S G
P I Q A Z L M R R U U E B K F N K P R F
D A W N E D O R D Q W H U L E B B R A P
C E S M B N N I S S I Y N G A O P O V A
P B Z N G P T V A U M T D C S R O V O L
I L Z A I S H E X J R L L T T N L I I A
R S C P H Z S T S Z H P E T O K G S R C
G B L S V R E Y U I E D L Z I S J I T E
L U Y P T R W W P R E Y U A J T O R E
U I A E G B C M P J E P I T S N B N A S
T B N U Q R O K L V I I T P V P W C V D
T W Y P H U E G I Q N C Y N A O M N E M
O H C I J R E R E Y B T O T E T Z R L T
N E E B E Y U N S D B S P V S S K Z E H
H U W C K K W K C T A Z T B T S P V R I
I R F Z Y L N C E H B J Y H O Y C P T R
I M P O S I T I O N E X E E R G I T L S
O R T I R O C I J B X D N U E P L J L T
P P E N S I O N M V T E E C X I T D N T
Y G T J E H O I A C H I N N U W U F V X
```

JEHOIACHIN	PALACE	STORE	MONTHS
PROVISION	PENSION	HEREIN	DEPICTS
POSITION	SUPPLIES	DAWNED	UNBORN
THIRST	QUENCHED	ARRIVE	SURPLUS
TRAVELER	BUNDLE	FEAST	GLUTTON

Evening

She was healed immediately.
—Luke 8:47

One of the most touching and teaching of the Savior's miracles is before us tonight. The woman was very ignorant. She imagined that virtue came out of Christ by a law of necessity, without His knowledge or direct will. Moreover, she was a stranger to the generosity of Jesus' character, or she would not have gone behind Him to steal the cure that He was so ready to give. Misery should always place itself right in the face of mercy. Had she known the love of Jesus' heart, she would have said, "I have but to put myself where He can see me. Then His omniscience will reveal my situation to Him, and His love will work my cure immediately." We admire her faith, but we marvel at her ignorance. After she had obtained the cure, she rejoiced with trembling. She was glad that the divine virtue had worked a miracle in her, but she feared lest Christ might retract the blessing and cancel the grant of His grace. Little did she comprehend the fullness of His love! We do not have as clear a view of Him as we could wish. We do not know the heights and depths of His love, but we know with certainty that He is too good to withdraw from a trembling soul the gift that it has been able to obtain. But here is the marvel of it: little as her knowledge was, her faith, because it was real faith, saved her, and saved her at once. There was no tedious delay—faith's miracle was instantaneous. If we have faith as a grain of mustard seed, salvation is our present and eternal possession. If, in the list of the Lord's children, we are written as the weakest of the family, yet, being heirs through faith, no power, human or devilish, can eject us from salvation. Even if we do not dare to lean our heads on His bosom as John did, yet we can venture into the crowd behind Him and touch the hem of His garment, and we will be made whole. Courage, timid one! Your faith has saved you. Go in peace. *"Being justified by faith, we have peace with God"* (Rom. 5:1).

```
D  B  M  S  X  M  I  R  A  C  L  E  S  F  S  F  R  C  N  N
D  E  C  I  U  Y  Z  G  W  V  J  I  P  S  T  Z  W  H  Q  S
A  H  I  U  M  T  U  N  N  P  I  Y  X  R  R  Z  A  X  C
G  I  S  A  R  A  X  I  W  O  L  V  O  Q  A  M  V  R  K  I
E  N  H  G  T  E  G  Q  E  L  R  T  L  U  N  O  N  A  A  F
N  D  J  D  O  K  V  I  D  V  F  A  W  I  G  R  H  C  M  C
E  U  T  O  U  C  H  I  N  G  D  D  N  U  E  E  T  T  P  B
R  R  T  L  Q  J  R  T  J  E  V  E  F  T  R  O  R  E  U  K
O  J  M  L  A  U  Z  Y  H  U  D  S  H  P  J  V  A  R  I  T
S  G  P  G  B  B  B  X  R  F  Z  X  S  L  U  P  E  W  Q  K  E
I  V  M  M  Y  P  T  Z  J  P  A  T  J  Q  Y  R  K  F  N  Z
T  O  M  N  I  S  C  I  E  N  C  E  T  E  X  M  W  A  O  T
Y  V  L  N  K  W  W  H  Q  T  D  A  A  V  U  F  M  E  W  H
T  R  E  M  B  L  I  N  G  D  U  L  M  I  S  E  R  Y  L  N
W  J  D  I  R  E  C  T  F  T  V  I  R  T  U  E  K  J  E  M
K  N  U  Y  N  J  V  Y  D  K  Y  H  W  I  L  L  H  Y  D  J
G  H  D  J  S  R  U  O  Z  L  T  Y  Q  U  C  D  L  V  G  Y
H  X  Q  O  N  E  C  E  S  S  I  T  Y  J  V  M  Z  F  E  T
X  Y  E  R  R  B  K  F  L  A  W  D  L  Z  M  A  M  P  H  F
K  R  W  K  Z  F  Z  M  K  F  X  L  N  Q  G  T  P  G  Q  D
```

TOUCHING	MIRACLES	IGNORANT	IMAGINED
VIRTUE	LAW	NECESSITY	KNOWLEDGE
DIRECT	WILL	MOREOVER	STRANGER
GENEROSITY	CHARACTER	BEHIND	STEAL
CURE	MISERY	OMNISCIENCE	TREMBLING

Morning

I will cause the shower to come down in his season;
there shall be showers of blessing.
—Ezekiel 34:26

Here is sovereign, divine mercy: "I will give them showers in their season." For who can say, "I will give them showers," except God? There is only one voice that can speak to the clouds and bid them to rain. Who sends down the rain upon the earth? Who scatters the showers upon the green herbs? Do not I, the Lord? So grace is the gift of God and is not created by man. It is also needed grace. What would the ground do without showers? You may break the clods; you may sow your seeds, but what can you do without the rain? As absolutely necessary is the divine blessing. In vain you labor, until God gives the plenteous shower and sends salvation down. Then it is plenteous grace. "I will send them showers." It does not say, "I will send them drops," but *"showers."* So it is with grace. If God gives a blessing, He usually gives it in such a measure that there is not room enough to receive it. Plenteous grace! Oh, we need plenteous grace to keep us humble, to make us prayerful, to make us holy; we need plenteous grace to make us zealous, to preserve us through this life, and at last to land us in heaven. We cannot do without saturating showers of grace. It is also seasonable grace. *"I will cause the shower to come down in his season."* What is your season this morning? Is it the season of drought? Then that is the season for showers. Is it a season of great heaviness and black clouds? Then that is the season for showers. *"As thy days, so shall thy strength be"* (Deut. 33:25). And here is a varied blessing. "I will give you *'showers'* of blessing." The word *"showers"* is in the plural. God will send all kinds of blessings. All God's blessings go together, like links in a golden chain. If He gives converting grace, He will also give comforting grace. He will send *"showers of blessing."* Look up today, O parched plant, and open your leaves and flowers for a heavenly watering.

```
Z E A L O U S W X N X V I B H Z H C D C
S A T U R A T I N G T T X U N D I L Z V
N O N Z N V P K Z Z T P M N M K E O F O
S V H Z E Z P L E N T E O U S B X U S I
N B E X C E P T Q G N S L I N K S D D C
E A R Q O H Q Q N F I I E T S K Q S O E
K L B N H F E P J H I G D A H U Q U C G
I C S S E L U A N Z L B N H S F R P N X
S E N O O Y U H V D T P O I U O K F C I
X M Z K J L N H A I K G N T Y S N N B Y
I K T J C C U Y A M N P S P P H K Y E D
M T V N C C J T H X Y E T I S O G H B I
N J I K X Z H H E P W J S X E W K D F G
R L X K T J T A L L M F C S E E Z R E D
T P A R C H E D I W Y J I O D R D O A C
G R E E N N O Z H N F F H S S W C U H L
P N W V E D I C A Q T J N K K R X G R O
C R A I N P L Y G G Y X T J D D M H D D
O B W N J R W D A B H V K T W H S T P S
J X E X Q Q Q K W R O O M U G J J K Z Y
```

SEASON	EXCEPT	VOICE	CLOUDS
RAIN	GREEN	HERBS	CLODS
SEEDS	ABSOLUTELY	PLENTEOUS	SHOWER
ROOM	ZEALOUS	SATURATING	DROUGHT
HEAVINESS	LINKS	CHAIN	PARCHED

Evening

O Lord of hosts, how long wilt thou not have mercy
on Jerusalem?…And the Lord answered the angel…
with good words and comfortable words.
—Zechariah 1:12–13

What a sweet answer to an anxious inquiry! This night let us rejoice in it. O Zion, there are good things in store for you. Your time of travail will soon be over. Your children will be brought forth, and your captivity will end. Patiently bear the rod for a season, and in the darkness still trust in God, for His love burns toward you. God loves the church with a love too deep for human imagination. He loves her with all His infinite heart; therefore, let her sons be of good courage. She cannot be far from prosperity to whom God speaks *"good words and comfortable words."* The prophet goes on to tell us what these comfortable words are: *"I am jealous for Jerusalem and for Zion with a great jealousy"* (Zech. 1:14). The Lord loves His church so much that He cannot bear that she would go astray to others; when she has done so, He cannot bear that she would suffer too much or too heavily. He will not have His enemies afflict her. He is displeased with them because they increase her misery. When God seems to have left His church, His heart is still warm toward her. History shows us that whenever God uses a rod to chasten His servants, He always breaks it afterward, as if He loathed the rod that gave His children pain. *"Like as a father pitieth his children, so the Lord pitieth them that fear him"* (Ps. 103:13). God has not forgotten us because He chastens us; His correction is no evidence of a lack of love. If this is true of His church collectively, it is also true of each individual member. You may fear that the Lord has passed you by, but that is not so. He who counts the stars and calls them by their names is in no danger of forgetting His own children. He knows your situation as thoroughly as if you were the only creature He ever made or the only saint He ever loved. Approach Him, and be at peace.

```
Z Y B H P J R F M V X F O R T H Z I A I
Z T I Z O R A T I P A T I E N T L Y L K
Z G S Q G V O N R U Y G X M V Y I U K V
D N I G H T J S S U F T M X X V M I B Q
T U W W Z H I D P W S L J D G Q A N T A
R B K D W G C F U E E T X M X C G C U Y
A B P R O P H E T S R R T X C O I G I T
V O Z A F S T S B S E I G T C M N Q X B
A C O K H Y Y D W Q G Z T P O F A K J K
I H L J Z N I J A I D O T Y U O T L U R
L U L F U U O F L R K H Q A R R I D D Z
M R A N X I O U S O K A Z I A T O V B I
P C E U I U L N S M P N E G G A N X V O
F H N P S Y C H N S K G E X E B W N B N
D J X S X Z W L N S F C S S W L A E E S
S U H C A P T I V I T Y E L S E L W A Y
Q K M I S Z N G N Z O W B J R W P X R Q
F E N L R V X T E K H U M A N A D M U V
M P K B W W N N W G T H H N B U R N S M
J E A L O U S A V G K Q A R Y J E W T X
```

ANSWER	ANXIOUS	NIGHT	ZION
TRAVAIL	FORTH	CAPTIVITY	PATIENTLY
BEAR	DARKNESS	TRUST	BURNS
CHURCH	HUMAN	IMAGINATION	COURAGE
PROSPERITY	COMFORTABLE	PROPHET	JEALOUS

Morning

Yea, he is altogether lovely.
—Song of Solomon 5:16

The superlative beauty of Jesus is all-attracting. It is not so much to be admired as to be loved. He is more than pleasant and fair; He is lovely. Surely the people of God can fully justify the use of this golden word, for He is the object of their warmest love, a love founded on the intrinsic excellence of His person, the complete perfection of His charms. O disciples of Jesus, look to your Master's lips and say, "Are they not most sweet?" Do not His words cause your hearts to burn within you as He talks with you by the way? Worshippers of Immanuel, look up to His head of much fine gold, and tell me, are not His thoughts precious to you? Is not your adoration sweetened with affection as you humbly bow before that countenance, which *"is as Lebanon, excellent as the cedars"* (Song 5:15)? Is there not a charm in His every feature, and is not His whole person fragrant with such a savor of His good ointments, that therefore the virgins love Him? Is there one member of His glorious body that is not attractive?—one portion of His person that is not a fresh lodestone to our souls?—one office that is not a strong cord to bind your heart? Our love is not as a seal set on His heart of love alone. It is fastened on His arm of power also. Nor is there a single part of Him on which it does not fix itself. We anoint His whole person with the sweet spikenard of our fervent love. His whole life we would imitate; His whole character we would copy. In all other beings we see some lack; in Him there is all perfection. Even the best of His favored saints have had blots on their garments and wrinkles on their brows. He is nothing but loveliness. All earthly suns have their spots. The fair world itself has its wilderness. We cannot love the whole of the loveliest thing, but Christ Jesus is gold without alloy, light without darkness, glory without cloud—*"Yea, he is altogether lovely."*

```
K P O C Y U T M D L T S Y Z N B W W P S
C H I V Z H E W R I N K L E S L I A G Y
G E F N O G L Y C M R E L R S O I J K D
Q I D O T N M S R K F L O E U T L A F G
T D E A D R V C U U W V V T P S G D Q L
K O M U R O I M M A N U E L E C X I V O
U J Y G Q S S N L O H P L B R M J S I R
G X T Z Z R F U S P D Q I T L B V C S I
Y V P N V H W E D I R G N L A S J I Y O
N C O U N T E N A N C E E Z T S E P W U
H P E R F E C T I O N W S N I M Q L S S
T X Q F E R V E N T Y R S A V F A E F N
L F E L F D W L E B A N O N E C J S D B
A R R O G O P N O R P L E A S A N T C G
Y L F B D G B S F T C S R G F H H D G P
F Y L C M S P I K E N A R D O C O R D B
N S O O E P B W Q Z D B F A N T O H B Y
Z F A V Y V B X X H L S G O L D E N G V
E A D O R A T I O N C F R A G R A N T I
I X N R T F K S D D K E E C M V M T K Z
```

SUPERLATIVE	PLEASANT	GOLDEN	INTRINSIC
DISCIPLES	IMMANUEL	ADORATION	COUNTENANCE
LEBANON	CEDARS	FRAGRANT	GLORIOUS
CORD	SPIKENARD	FERVENT	PERFECTION
BLOTS	WRINKLES	LOVELINESS	ALLOY

41

Evening

Abide in me.
—John 15:4

Communion with Christ is a certain cure for every ill. Whether it is bitter sorrow or excessive pleasure, close fellowship with the Lord Jesus will remove the pain from the one and the imbalance from the other. Live near to Jesus, Christian, and it is matter of secondary importance whether you reside on the mountain of honor or in the valley of humiliation. Living near to Jesus, you are covered with the wings of God; underneath you are the *"everlasting arms"* (Deut. 33:27). Let nothing keep you from that hallowed fellowship, which is the choice privilege of a soul wedded to the Lord. Do not be content with an interview now and then, but always seek to retain His company. Only in His presence will you find either comfort or safety. Jesus should not be a friend who calls upon us now and then, but One with whom we walk continuously. Do you have a difficult road before you? O traveler to heaven, see that you do not go without your Guide. Do you have to pass through the fiery furnace? Do not enter it unless, like Shadrach, Meshach, and Abednego, you have the Son of God as your Companion. Do you have to battle the Jericho of your own sins? Then do not attempt the warfare until, like Joshua, you have seen the Captain of the Lord's host with His sword drawn in His hand. Are you called to meet the Esau of your many temptations? Do not meet him until at Jabbok's brook you have laid hold on the angel and have prevailed. In every case, in every condition, you will need Jesus. When the iron gates of death open, you will need Him most of all. Keep close to your soul's Husband. Lean your head on His breast, and ask to be refreshed with the spiced wine of His pomegranate. Then you will be found by Him at the end, without *"spot, or wrinkle, or any such thing"* (Eph. 5:27). Since you have lived with Him and lived in Him here, you will abide with Him forever.

```
I C T A X B D Y W B M E S H R Y C U H L
E T H M B E Q M T I E X R U Z J N D S D
B L I R G E W H B T S C Q M I J G T J X
V O L U I Y D U K T H E U I Y Q S E F S
A C E L W S H N E E A S B L A C W V G P
L D D M H P T X E R C S D I N S Q E W I
L F U R N A C E O G H I I A V U K R D C
E P L E A S U R E U O V M T W K F L X E
Y A I Q E O I F I X D E B I W L I A P D
K P O M E G R A N A T E A O G L T S Q S
H S Q S O R R O W P K T L N J A V T P A
M Q J S X N S C W H T J A D I I M I T F
B T N V T Q N V Z F W N N V M T Q N J E
X X F Q O E A Y K D J S C T T L C G T T
I M P O R T A N C E L T E J Y J I K G Y
R H D H N C O N T I N U O U S L Y L Y O
Y Z N M T W Q S L Z U P P K A Z T Y R F
H L Q R D A M B H M O U N T A I N Y N E
J S E C O N D A R Y K S B W R W Q O X R
F H D O S C S H A D R A C H Z N U K X Z
```

CHRIST   BITTER   SORROW   EXCESSIVE

PLEASURE   IMBALANCE   SECONDARY   IMPORTANCE

MOUNTAIN   VALLEY   HUMILIATION   EVERLASTING

SAFETY   CONTINUOUSLY   FURNACE   SHADRACH

MESHACH   ABEDNEGO   SPICED   POMEGRANATE

Morning

Sin…exceeding sinful.
—Romans 7:13

Beware of frivolous thoughts of sin. At the time of conversion, the conscience is so tender that we are afraid of the slightest sin. Young converts have a holy timidity, a godly fear lest they should offend God. But alas! Very soon the fine bloom on these first ripe fruits is removed by the rough handling of the surrounding world. The sensitive plant of young piety turns into a willow in later life; it grows too pliant, too easily yielding. By degrees men become familiar with sin. The ear in which the cannon has been booming will not notice slight sounds. At first a little sin startles us; but soon, we say, "Is it not a little one?" Then there comes a larger one, and then another, until by degrees we begin to regard sin as but a little transgression. Then follows an unholy presumption: "We have not fallen into open sin. True, we tripped a little, but we stood upright on the whole. We may have uttered one unholy word, but most of our conversation has been consistent." So we excuse sin. We throw a cloak over it and call it by dainty names. Christian, beware of thinking lightly of sin. Take heed lest you fall little by little. Sin, a little thing? Is it not a poison? Who knows its deadliness? Sin, a little thing? Do not the little foxes spoil the grapes (Song 2:15)? Does not the tiny coral insect build a rock that wrecks a navy? Do not little strokes fell lofty oaks? Will not droplets of water eventually wear away stones? Sin, a little thing? It circled the Redeemer's head with thorns and pierced His heart! It made Him suffer anguish, bitterness, and woe. If you could weigh the least sin on the scales of eternity, you would fly from it as from a serpent and abhor the least appearance of evil. Look on all sin as that which crucified the Savior, and you will see it to be *"exceeding sinful."*

```
N S E N S I T I V E L E T L T S A P X Z
Y I A F V P Z N X H Y Q Q C E L M K Y M
S A N N Z S M N I Q L A U Z D I Z P N K
H A T S S I I B B Z P T Z C N G N L Q N
P V X I J N E Q A E I Y X Q G H T A S G
C K G Q M W A V F E E N E D S T R N U S
X Z O W D I R G J L T X A L L E A T R B
Y O D D V C D A A B Y H B E H S N U R T
X L L K Z N X I T H O U G H T T S I O G
N J Y K D A I N T Y M H C A A J G G U I
W D W E N O F Y S Y M H P F P V R I N U
X M Q H W Y N R M B V S N D N O E B D A
B E K N Y L O G A W M M Y L G F S X I L
F T F B M Q U Q X I X E X Q H F S W N A
U P R I G H T B I P D C M T C E I S G S
Z D Z L J P B J D C X J J Y A N O B M N
J J B E W A R E U A U E E U Z D N D H X
F R U I T S M F E T H A O B L O O M Z G
H H J A C O N V E R S I O N D B Y U J I
I I P S D T E N D E R L U Z B R R S Y K
```

BEWARE	THOUGHT	CONVERSION	TENDER
AFRAID	SLIGHTEST	SIN	TIMIDITY
GODLY	OFFEND	ALAS	BLOOM
FRUITS	SURROUNDING	SENSITIVE	PLANT
PIETY	TRANSGRESSION	UPRIGHT	DAINTY

Evening

Thou shalt be called, Sought out.
—Isaiah 62:12

The surpassing grace of God is seen very clearly in that we were not only sought, but *"sought out."* Men seek for something that has been lost on the floor of the house, but in such a situation, there is only seeking, not seeking out. The loss is more perplexing and the search more persevering when a thing is sought out. We were mingled with the mire. It is as if we were like some precious piece of gold that had fallen into a sewer. Men gather together to carefully inspect the mass of abominable filth, and they continue to stir and rake and search among the heap until the treasure is found. Or, to use another example, we were lost in a maze. We wandered here and there, and when mercy came after us with the Gospel, it did not find us at the first coming. It had to search for us and seek us out, for like lost sheep, we were so desperately lost. We had wandered into a strange country, and it did not seem possible that even the Good Shepherd would be able to follow our devious wanderings. Glory be to unconquerable grace: we were sought out! No gloom could hide us; no filthiness could conceal us. We were found and brought home. Glory be to infinite love: God the Holy Spirit restored us! If the lives of some of God's people could be written, they would fill us with holy astonishment. Strange and marvelous are the ways that God used in their cases to find His own. Blessed be His name! He never relinquishes the search until the chosen are sought out. They are not a people sought today and cast away tomorrow. Almightiness and wisdom combined will make no failures. They will be called, *"Sought out."* That any should be sought out is matchless grace, but that we should be sought out is grace beyond degree! We can find no reason for it but God's own sovereign love. We can only lift up our hearts in wonder and praise the Lord that this night we wear the name *"Sought out."*

```
I  J  T  L  S  X  D  V  A  U  B  P  D  A  G  L  Q  G  H  O
H  X  S  R  M  O  N  C  F  Q  Y  E  O  B  F  Q  F  X  D  P
Z  M  R  N  E  C  U  G  F  W  B  R  F  O  X  C  Y  C  F  K
U  L  A  H  Y  A  M  G  N  L  N  S  K  M  M  I  T  X  R  Q
I  N  A  Z  X  G  S  M  H  Q  I  E  F  I  C  Q  N  J  O  B
O  O  C  K  E  D  D  U  K  T  D  R  L  N  U  Y  U  D  L  Y
H  S  U  O  F  O  N  K  R  J  G  V  O  A  U  R  U  S  S  Z
H  E  D  M  N  K  M  V  X  E  U  E  O  B  F  N  A  U  U  N
F  O  A  Q  I  Q  T  D  U  V  W  R  R  L  Z  I  L  K  F  F
S  R  U  P  O  R  U  Y  O  S  O  I  I  E  L  H  I  F  E  S
V  P  N  S  T  L  E  E  C  W  W  N  U  L  R  Y  N  I  M  U
K  J  F  T  E  V  J  A  R  Y  K  G  P  K  W  K  S  L  L  R
Y  Y  B  U  Y  S  I  T  U  A  T  I  O  N  C  O  P  T  X  P
S  L  B  W  A  N  G  K  I  U  B  K  C  B  B  C  E  H  V  A
X  I  S  L  N  P  C  P  G  K  R  L  V  A  V  E  C  Q  F  S
Z  G  O  S  P  E  L  H  R  P  L  O  E  E  S  K  T  H  A  S
M  G  L  O  O  M  A  F  E  A  N  B  I  Y  U  T  I  N  L  I
E  E  S  L  E  O  N  R  S  E  W  E  R  I  T  S  J  G  D  N
K  C  K  S  L  W  Q  P  G  O  R  Y  U  Z  D  K  S  T  A  G
Q  P  C  E  C  V  T  D  D  E  S  P  E  R  A  T  E  L  Y  X
```

SURPASSING	SOUGHT	FLOOR	HOUSE
SITUATION	PERSEVERING	MIRE	SEWER
INSPECT	ABOMINABLE	FILTH	RAKE
HEAP	TREASURE	MAZE	GOSPEL
DESPERATELY	UNCONQUERABLE	GLOOM	CAST

Morning

Ye shall be scattered, every man to his own,
and shall leave me alone.
—John 16:32

Few had fellowship with the sorrows of Gethsemane. The majority of the disciples were not sufficiently advanced in grace to be admitted to behold the mysteries of His *"agony"* (Luke 22:44). Occupied with the Passover Feast at their own houses, they represent the many who live on the letter, but are mere babes as to the spirit of the Gospel. To the Twelve, no, to eleven only, was the privilege given to enter Gethsemane and see this great sight. Out of the eleven, eight were left at a distance; they had fellowship, but not of that intimate sort to which men greatly beloved are admitted. Only three highly favored ones could approach the veil of our Lord's mysterious sorrow. Within that veil, even these must not intrude; a stone's throw distance must be left between. He must tread *"the winepress alone"* (Isa. 63:3), and of the people there must be none with Him. Peter and the two sons of Zebedee represent the few eminent, experienced saints who may be written down as "Fathers." Having done business on great waters, they can, in some degree, measure the huge Atlantic waves of their Redeemer's passion. To some selected spirits it is given, for the good of others, and to strengthen them for future, special, and tremendous conflict, to enter the inner circle and hear the pleadings of the suffering High Priest. They have fellowship with Him in His sufferings and are made conformable unto His death (Phil. 3:10). Yet even these cannot penetrate the secret places of the Savior's woe. "Thine unknown sufferings" is the remarkable expression of the Greek liturgy. There was an inner room in our Master's grief, shut out from human knowledge and fellowship. There Jesus was left alone. Here Jesus was more than ever an *"unspeakable gift"* (2 Cor. 9:15). Was not Watts right when he penned, "And all the unknown joys He gives were bought with agonies unknown"?

```
F P B U V G R E E K N U F C S C B R L M
O N G E M R B A B E S M A H B J P M N L
Z P M E L J W F X E C W V W H R Y Y X E
T M L A T O Y T L L P Z O U G I Y S W A
Q C E E J H V T M T D S R D A C I T A Q
S Z B Q A O S E R T B X E E T L N E D E
A F J P S D R E D S U H D C L Z T R V R
E G A D A S I I M B E I P H A I I A T
N J O F F U H N T A M Q P D N E M E N I
O Q D N B D T I G Y N A A X T E A S C U
U G Q Z Y I M K G S T E S N I Q T X E G
E F M Z P S M Y U H S S S U C C E V D T
S D X C I T T W I T L F O N H Q X E D V
Y A S T O A K Z O K F Y V Y I E G A C T
U W Y Y Z N L E E L F Q E R C G M B V O
R C D R S C A F L I T U R G Y K X S X Z
X Y B L T E W O D Y B Q W C G G V R T I
V E I L Y M S U F F I C I E N T L Y A V
N A D M I T T E D N S W N O U Z U Q Q G
Q Z Y I U L D G A P P R O A C H S G V U
```

GETHSEMANE   MAJORITY   SUFFICIENTLY   ADVANCED
MYSTERIES   AGONY   PASSOVER   BABES
DISTANCE   INTIMATE   BELOVED   ADMITTED
HIGHLY   FAVORED   APPROACH   VEIL
ATLANTIC   PLEADINGS   GREEK   LITURGY

Evening

Canst thou bind the sweet influences of Pleiades,
or loose the bands of Orion?
—Job 38:31

If we are inclined to boast of our abilities, the grandeur of nature may soon show us how puny we are. We cannot move the least of all the twinkling stars or quench even one of the beams of the morning. We speak of power, but the heavens laugh us to scorn. When the Pleiades, a magnificent cluster of stars, shine forth in the spring with new joy, we cannot restrain their influences, and when Orion reigns aloft, and the year is bound in winter's fetters, we cannot relax the icy bands. The seasons revolve according to divine appointment. The whole race of men cannot change their schedule. Lord, what is man? In the spiritual, as in the natural world, man's power is limited on all sides. When the Holy Spirit sheds abroad His delights in the soul, nothing can take away that joy. All the cunning and malice of men are ineffective in halting the life-giving power of the Comforter. When He deigns to visit a church and revive it, the most inveterate enemies cannot resist the good work; they may ridicule it, but they can no more restrain it than they can push back the spring when the Pleiades rule the hour. God wills it, and so it must be. On the other hand, if the Lord in sovereignty or in justice binds up a man so that his soul is in bondage, who can give him liberty? God alone can remove the winter of spiritual death from an individual or a people. He looses the bands of Orion, and no one but He can do that. What a blessing it is that He can do it! Oh, that He would perform the wonder tonight! Lord, end my winter, and let my spring begin. In spite of all my desires to do so, I cannot raise my soul out of her death and dullness, but all things are possible with You. I need celestial influences, the clear shinings of Your love, the beams of Your grace, the light of Your countenance—these are the Pleiades to me. I suffer from sin and temptation—these are my wintry signs, my terrible Orion. Lord, work wonders in me and for me. Amen.

```
C E Z C I J Z A H S K T L T T F F F Y M
N C E U B N M W Q E K Z G R N T B J L A
S P R I N G C X Q B K Q I V X W X F F G
G Q A H T S L L R F S F L N V I W L K N
Q P I A W K O L I Z J F Z O U N G J G I
N U A T E Y W L G N I L D T O K L H M F
I N F L U E N C E S E U B J R L Z H T I
N Y L C S S V C U J A D T T I I M P C C
E Z O R L N W D L P I D Y Q O N J G U E
O N N H N S T O I U L P V K N G W P N N
P H H D T Z T Z I G S O I X L G R B N T
M K A Z T T H A S N C T S H L R Y P I M
U J L I Z K R H R O B M E K T A T L N L
X A O J C P Q F A S M J V R H N H E G Z
G O F G V Y B A S T X S G F V D F I D U
M Z T E N N O N L T F C H T K E M A B A
T E H D J O A T B A N D S I W U K D B F
F E T T E R S Q O I X S Z W N R Y E D G
W A F J V R T M C H Y G U F J E T S G E
J B E A M S A C A B I L I T I E S S C W
```

INCLINED	BOAST	ABILITIES	GRANDEUR
PUNY	TWINKLING	STARS	BEAMS
PLEIADES	MAGNIFICENT	CLUSTER	SHINE
SPRING	INFLUENCES	ORION	ALOFT
FETTERS	ICY	BANDS	CUNNING

Morning

Betrayest thou the Son of man with a kiss?
—Luke 22:48

The kisses of an enemy are deceitful. Let me be on my guard when the world puts on a loving face, for it will, if possible, betray me as it did my Master—with a kiss. Whenever a man is about to attack religion, he usually professes very great reverence for it. Let me beware of the sleek-faced hypocrisy that is the armor-bearer to heresy and infidelity. Knowing the deceptiveness of unrighteousness, let me be wise as a serpent to detect and avoid the designs of the enemy. The *"young man void of understanding"* (Prov. 7:7) was led astray by the kiss of the strange woman. May my soul be so graciously instructed all this day that the *"much fair speech"* (v. 21) of the world may have no effect on me. Holy Spirit, let me not, a poor frail son of man, be betrayed with a kiss! But what if I would be guilty of the same accursed sin as Judas, that *"son of perdition"* (John 17:12)? I have been baptized into the name of the Lord Jesus; I am a member of His visible church; I sit at the Communion table—all these are like so many kisses from my lips. Am I sincere in them? If not, I am a base traitor. Do I live in the world as carelessly as others do and yet make a profession of being a follower of Jesus? If so, I expose religion to ridicule and lead men to speak evil of the holy name by which I am called. Surely if I act thus inconsistently, I am a Judas, and it would be better for me if I *"had never been born"* (Mark 14:21). Dare I hope that I am clear in this matter? Then, O Lord, keep me so. O Lord, make me sincere and true. Preserve me from every false way. Never let me betray my Savior. I love You, Jesus, and though I often grieve You, yet I desire to abide faithful even to death. O God, forbid that I would be a high-soaring professor of faith, and then fall at last into the lake of fire because I betrayed my Master with a kiss.

```
M I N C A X O Y O K F K M O U V B V C Z
R M A S T E R D Q O M Y T M D Y K L N K
F J A X T A C C U R S E D A E F Z Z D Z
Z Z N H A B T L A E Y T X Y C A I G E C
B W V K C H E J M S S P D E E Y J D C G
G C F G K Q R T R W T O O U I V D E E P
P U V V X S C S R E H J H S T K P S P E
X O A H E I V E I A C E Z U F I V I T R
R S S R R T K R J Y Y C N R U S J G I D
E R C S D A P P X K J L B E L S B N V I
L C R J I U X E D X A D L U V Z E S E T
I K L G U B J N F B E V J G F E I B N I
G G B W N B L T S L A X C X E G R M E O
I Z A N V E I E I V X M H T N N T H S N
O K W B M M T I N F I D E L I T Y V S X
N I L R Y R J U D A S U R B N U B I V W
Q H M Y K K J E G D V X E Q U Y F S O T
R E V E R E N C E Q I Q S Y F W P Q C H
P R O F E S S E S K P X Y Z D V Q I G H
M V C H X B F W I E N E M Y C M B S B O
```

ENEMY	DECEITFUL	GUARD	POSSIBLE
BETRAY	MASTER	KISS	WHENEVER
ATTACK	RELIGION	PROFESSES	REVERENCE
HERESY	INFIDELITY	DECEPTIVENESS	SERPENT
DESIGNS	ACCURSED	JUDAS	PERDITION

Evening

The Son of man.
—John 3:13

How constantly our Master used the title, the *"Son of man"*! If He had chosen, He could have always spoken of Himself as the Son of God, *"Wonderful, Counsellor, The mighty God, The everlasting Father, The Prince of Peace"* (Isa. 9:6). But behold the lowliness of Jesus! He prefers to call Himself the *"Son of man."* Let us learn a lesson of humility from our Savior. Let us never court great titles or proud degrees. There is here, however, a far sweeter thought. Jesus loved mankind so much that He delighted to honor it; since it is a high honor, indeed, the greatest dignity of mankind, that Jesus is the Son of Man. He desires to display this name so that He may, as it were, hang royal stars upon the breast of humanity and show forth the love of God to Abraham's seed. *"Son of man"*—whenever He said those words, He placed a halo around the head of Adam's children. Yet there is perhaps a more precious thought that remains. Jesus Christ called Himself the *"Son of man"* in order to express His oneness and sympathy with His people. He thus reminds us that He is the One whom we may approach without fear. We may take all our griefs and troubles to Him, for, as a Man, He knows them by experience. In that He Himself has suffered as the *"Son of man,"* He is able to help and to comfort us. All hail, blessed Jesus! Inasmuch as You are forever using the sweet name that acknowledges that You are a Brother and a close relative, it is to us a dear token of Your grace, Your humility, and Your love.

> Oh, see how Jesus trusts Himself
>   Unto our childish love,
> As though by His free ways with us
>   Our earnestness to prove!
> His sacred name a common word
>   On earth He loves to hear;
> There is no majesty in Him
>   Which love may not come near.

```
A  T  S  W  E  E  T  E  R  G  N  X  H  P  H  I  Z  D  V  S
W  X  J  G  H  I  X  L  Q  K  W  H  R  U  G  M  F  E  E  P
C  O  U  R  T  Q  M  N  S  K  F  H  Q  Z  P  Y  O  G  P  O
H  W  N  X  Y  X  H  L  E  S  S  O  N  Q  G  G  N  R  F  K
T  A  R  R  Z  J  D  K  A  I  U  N  E  M  G  S  E  E  F  E
A  B  R  A  H  A  M  X  N  L  Q  H  A  R  H  U  N  E  W  N
Y  D  I  S  P  L  A  Y  G  W  W  M  B  W  K  D  E  S  G  W
W  D  K  B  F  N  N  J  S  B  U  A  Z  W  D  Q  S  L  O  M
D  V  B  K  B  A  W  I  S  Q  T  G  Y  Z  E  A  S  L  J  A
R  Q  M  H  A  L  O  H  Y  Q  C  R  D  S  B  Y  L  Y  Q  N
E  P  D  O  T  T  S  X  M  W  F  O  I  N  K  F  O  N  H  K
F  D  U  L  I  N  P  O  P  E  Q  H  G  E  V  O  W  A  I  I
G  H  S  B  T  P  B  J  A  L  P  V  N  F  A  E  L  T  M  N
X  V  Y  H  L  N  M  D  T  W  G  R  I  S  P  Y  I  I  S  D
X  T  Y  A  E  M  N  I  H  V  D  L  T  A  L  N  N  A  E  V
A  B  M  M  T  A  G  C  Y  N  U  F  Y  V  P  K  E  K  L  L
L  T  C  O  U  N  S  E  L  L  O  R  M  I  A  V  S  N  F  Q
J  C  O  N  S  T  A  N  T  L  Y  U  Q  O  A  U  S  E  A  S
W  W  R  L  C  E  N  P  A  B  T  U  J  R  H  C  Z  P  E  X
L  W  O  N  D  E  R  F  U  L  W  U  C  S  V  Q  Q  D  O  N
```

CONSTANTLY	TITLE	ALWAYS	SPOKEN
HIMSELF	WONDERFUL	COUNSELLOR	LOWLINESS
LESSON	SAVIOR	COURT	DEGREES
SWEETER	MANKIND	DIGNITY	DISPLAY
ABRAHAM	HALO	ONENESS	SYMPATHY

Morning

He answered him to never a word.
—Matthew 27:14

He was never slow of speech when He could bless the sons of men, but He would not say a single word for Himself. *"Never man spake like this man"* (John 7:46), and never was any man silent like Him. Was this singular silence the indication of His perfect self-sacrifice? Did it show that He would not utter a word to stop the slaughter of His sacred person, which He had dedicated as an offering for us? Had He so entirely surrendered Himself that He would not interfere in His own behalf, even in the minutest degree, but be bound and slain a submissive, uncomplaining victim? Was this silence a type of the defenselessness of sin? Nothing can be said to lessen or excuse human guilt; therefore, He who bore its whole weight stood speechless before His judge. Is not patient silence the best reply to a contentious world? Calm endurance answers some questions infinitely more conclusively than the loftiest eloquence. The best apologists for Christianity in the early days were its martyrs. The anvil breaks a host of hammers by quietly bearing their blows. Did not the silent Lamb of God furnish us with a grand example of wisdom? Where every word was occasion for new blasphemy, it was the line of duty to afford no fuel for the flame of sin. The ambiguous and the false, the unworthy and the contemptible, will before long overthrow and destroy themselves; therefore, the true can afford to be quiet and find silence to be their wisdom. Evidently our Lord, by His silence, furnished a remarkable fulfillment of prophecy. A long defense of Himself would have been contrary to Isaiah's prediction. *"He is brought as a lamb to the slaughter, and as a sheep before her shearers is dumb, so he openeth not his mouth"* (Isa. 53:7). By His quiet, He conclusively proved Himself to be the true Lamb of God. As such we salute Him this morning. Be with us, Jesus, and in the silence of our hearts, let us hear the voice of Your love.

```
W Z C L M B V S J S L O W E G T C O W I
T A G H D I S J B O U N D N K F D O E N
B E H A L F N I A E S L M T Z G E B I T
G S B A S L S U L L Q T F I Z K D D N E
E A A C Q L Y K T E J I B R S L I E D R
Z K Q P E N A Z G E N A F E X T C L I F
D N M M Z S N I Z D S C N L Y D A O C E
E Z M H T Z L P N L R T E Y W Z T Q A R
I R Y W X O J W D J G L Y O A S E U T E
S L O B S X X S I N G U L A R H D E I C
U N C O M P L A I N I N G N J E S N O K
T E G W G T Y U M M R I D J C A Q C N H
O I S U R R E N D E R E D E K R M E K X
C K Z C N A F F L C N S K U K E W V R R
D S U B M I S S I V E S B Z M R K I Q A
P Y F D E V A C E F T T L S J S F C H X
W L S I M V D N G U L C E F P G L T F R
X Z U V Z W C X V G D O S X H B I I Z J
S A C R E D M T T A A V S V M S U M K K
I R S V G R C D U G S L A U G H T E R B
```

SLOW	BLESS	SINGULAR	SILENCE
INDICATION	SLAUGHTER	SACRED	DEDICATED
ENTIRELY	SURRENDERED	INTERFERE	BEHALF
MINUTEST	BOUND	SLAIN	SUBMISSIVE
UNCOMPLAINING	VICTIM	ELOQUENCE	SHEARERS

Evening

He shall see his seed, he shall prolong his days, and the pleasure
of the LORD shall prosper in his hand.
—Isaiah 53:10

All you who love the Lord, plead for the speedy fulfillment of the promise of today's text. It is easy work to pray when our desires are grounded in and based on God's own promise. How can He who gave the Word refuse to keep it? Unchangeable truth cannot demean itself by a lie, and eternal faithfulness cannot degrade itself by neglect. God must bless His Son; His covenant binds Him to it. What the Spirit prompts us to ask from Jesus is that which God decrees to give to Him. Whenever you are praying for the kingdom of Christ, let your eyes behold the dawning of the blessed day that is drawing near, when the Crucified One will receive His crown in the place where men rejected Him. Be encouraged, you who prayerfully work and toil for Christ with little apparent success. It will not always be so. Better times are ahead for you. Your eyes cannot see the blissful future. Borrow the telescope of faith, wipe the misty breath of your doubts from the glass, look through it, and see the coming glory. Reader, do you make this your constant prayer? Remember that the same Christ who told us to say, *"Give us this day our daily bread"* (Matt. 6:11), first gave us this petition: *"Hallowed be thy name. Thy kingdom come. Thy will be done in earth, as it is in heaven"* (vv. 9–10). Do not let your prayers be all about your own sins, your own needs, your own imperfections, or your own trials. Instead, let them climb the starry ladder and reach Christ Himself. Then, as you draw near to the blood-sprinkled mercy seat, offer this prayer continually: "Lord, extend the kingdom of Your dear Son." Such a petition, fervently presented, will elevate the spirit of all your devotions. Remember that you prove the sincerity of your prayer by working to promote the Lord's glory.

```
R U Q Q P E D S Z T R A P P Y Y B I W S
J Z I C R N V C G W H R E J E C T E D D
V L U Y O G R A H R H R S F H I K M L E
U U P R M M Y T E L E S C O P E D Y F M
E C R P P E J J G R O U N D E D E V A E
V J A G T X V U S K K D N N X E G P I A
V I Y S S Z P B P P C E B S J O R A T N
L T O J T P S L V T W C O B S P A I H U
M I S T Y P F G O L L R S S Q H D G F W
Y L H P D H V N Y R T E U A J D E U U N
B D E I G X P S T R D E Z O D O J T L O
Z L U B W Q G K Q Z Z S G X C U T R N M
C R I K S L T X K J E F R P I B R P E T
Y X G D N B A I J L D D Q E O T F Q S P
M F U L F I L L M E N T S I F S B Z S Q
U N C H A N G E A B L E Y F V U Y W Y U
N G O I I M C R U C I F I E D H S C X B
T O A N F Z G K K W W R M B Y I D E J F
Q K T E X T X I B I N D S A G L A S S X
Y C H A L L O W E D E S V Y A A K W P J
```

LORD	FULFILLMENT	TEXT	PRAY
GROUNDED	REFUSE	UNCHANGEABLE	DEMEAN
FAITHFULNESS	DEGRADE	BINDS	PROMPTS
DECREES	CRUCIFIED	REJECTED	TELESCOPE
MISTY	DOUBTS	GLASS	HALLOWED

Morning

They took Jesus, and led him away.
—John 19:16

He had been in agony all night. After spending the early morning at the hall of Caiaphas, He had been hurried from Caiaphas to Pilate, from Pilate to Herod, and from Herod back again to Pilate. He had, therefore, but little strength left, and yet neither refreshment nor rest were permitted Him. They were eager for His blood, so they led Him out to die, bearing the weight of the cross. O heartbreaking procession! Well may the daughters of peace weep. My soul, weep also. What do we learn here as we see our blessed Lord led forth? Do we not perceive that truth that was foreshadowed by the scapegoat? Did not the high priest bring the scapegoat and put both his hands on its head, confessing the sins of the people, so that those sins might be laid on the goat and be removed from the people? Then the man selected to lead the goat took it into the wilderness, and it carried away the sins of the people, so that if they were sought for, they could not be found. Now we see Jesus brought before the priests and rulers, who pronounce Him guilty. God Himself places the blame for our sins on Him: *"The Lord hath laid on him the iniquity of us all"* (Isa. 53:6); *"He hath made him to be sin for us"* (2 Cor. 5:21). As the substitute for our guilt, bearing our sin—represented by the cross—on His shoulders, the great Scapegoat was led away by the appointed officers of justice. Beloved, can you feel assured that He carried *your* sin? As you look at the cross on His shoulders, does it represent *your* sin? There is one way by which you can tell whether He carried your sin or not. Have you laid your hand on His head, confessed your sin, and trusted in Him? Then your sin no longer lies on you; it has all been transferred by blessed imputation to Christ, and He bears it on His shoulder as a load heavier than the cross. Do not let the picture vanish until you have rejoiced in your own deliverance and adored the loving Redeemer on whom your iniquities were laid.

```
M F S Y H K E C J B V R R O E Z B T Y P
C H O I E H B N R P R O C E S S I O N P
D O U R E F E Q G A O M O R N I N G E D
D P N B E C J A I Z T K G E W W P Q F A
X E E F D S O F R D D D B H L S R D P U
Y W R R E U H I R T P S M Y U A O P H G
W K A Q M S N A F U B O X H Y W N Q B H
E P N H H I S W D G Y R I P S P O F G T
I Y B J E J T I I O K K E B A Q U V C E
G L Y D K R Z T N L W I X A J F N G A R
H X S K H S O A E G D E L H K B C F I S
T S C Q I S U D I D W E D N G I E G A P
G W A D W R R N P D F I R Z Q U N V P M
W C P V A M B Z Q N J X Z N P Z V G H Q
E S E L E C T E D P I L A T E V C L A P
A J G J S A I N I Q U I T Y Y S F I S D
G A O Z U H G V U R M N B W R S S P V B
E U A G H D V N B T X I T R U T H I F Z
R D T F F O C Q B X B E A R I N G A S U
Q R P C I V S M B R U L E R S C Q T B V
```

MORNING CAIAPHAS PILATE HEROD
PERMITTED EAGER BEARING WEIGHT
HEARTBREAKING PROCESSION DAUGHTERS TRUTH
FORESHADOWED SCAPEGOAT CONFESSING SELECTED
WILDERNESS RULERS PRONOUNCE INIQUITY

Evening

All we like sheep have gone astray; we have turned every one to his own way; and the
Lord hath laid on him the iniquity of us all.
—Isaiah 53:6

This confession of sin is common to all the elect people of God. We have all fallen; therefore, in common chorus, from the first who entered heaven to the last who will enter there, we can all say, *"All we like sheep have gone astray."* The confession, while unanimous, is also unique and individual: *"We have turned every one to his own way."* There is a particular sinfulness about every person. All are sinful, but each one has some special aggravation not found in others. It is the mark of genuine repentance that it naturally associates itself with other penitents, but it also takes up a position of individuality. *"We have turned every one to his own way"* is a confession that each person has sinned against light in a way unique to himself or sinned with an intensity that he does not perceive in others. This confession is also unreserved. There is not a word to detract from its force or a syllable by way of excuse. The confession is a giving up of all pleas of self-righteousness. It is the declaration of those who are consciously guilty— guilty with severity, guilty without excuse. They stand with their weapons of rebellion broken in pieces and cry, *"All we like sheep have gone astray; we have turned every one to his own way."* Yet we hear no mournful wailing attending this confession of sin, for the next sentence makes it almost a song: *"The Lord hath laid on him the iniquity of us all."* It is the most grievous sentence of the three, but it overflows with comfort. It is strange that where misery was con-centrated, mercy reigned; where sorrow reached her climax, weary souls find rest. The bruised Savior is the Healer of bruised hearts. See how the lowliest repentance gives place to assured confidence through simply gazing at Christ on the cross!

```
I E E I G I Z J U L I N T E N S I T Y H
N U O O F E T V R W P A L K C M C C O E
D A F Z F X B M D T A K S T G V W O U L
I Q I P Y C E W R X R E S T K U K N U E
V W R D W R K T P C T E I W R U V F F C
I J S V A B S R U O I G N T P A P E V T
D P T X I Y F G N M C D F R I O Y S T N
U L S P E C I A L M U J U C V B F S I H
A Z A C P H N Q A O L D L G T V N I C O
L R B S E E T K R N A V N E M V O O I R
I Q Z U T Q O I N S R N E N Z V Q N N Y
T K W H P V C P Z I P O S U Y O L C D H
Y Q G C M A Q J L C Z Y S I Q L U Q I Q
L Z D G S R L I B E C N Q N I P M N V M
P Y A G G R A V A T I O N E M W R Q I Q
S R O R M G R E P E N T A N C E Q P D I
U N A N I M O U S W W J Z F T G S Y U X
B S M M P J P F A L L E N P S V P H A K
Z T B G P K G K K U N I Q U E N O A L S
R H G L Q S F Z Q R T K C H O R U S Y I
```

CONFESSION	ELECT	PEOPLE	FALLEN
COMMON	CHORUS	FIRST	LAST
ASTRAY	UNANIMOUS	UNIQUE	INDIVIDUAL
PARTICULAR	SINFULNESS	SPECIAL	AGGRAVATION
GENUINE	REPENTANCE	INDIVIDUALITY	INTENSITY

Morning

Him hath God exalted.
—Acts 5:31

Jesus, our Lord, once crucified, dead, and buried, now sits on the throne of glory. The highest place that heaven affords is His by undisputed right. It is sweet to remember that the exaltation of Christ in heaven is a representative exaltation. He is exalted at the Father's right hand, and though as Jehovah He had eminent glories in which finite creatures cannot share, yet as the Mediator, the honors that Jesus wears in heaven are the heritage of all the saints. It is delightful to reflect how close Christ's union is with His people. We are actually one with Him. We are members of His body, and His exaltation is our exaltation. He has a crown, and He gives us crowns, too. He will give us places of honor, even as He has overcome, and is set down with His Father on His throne. He is not content with having a throne to Himself. On His right hand, there must be His queen, arrayed *"in gold of Ophir"* (Ps. 45:9). He cannot be glorified without His bride. Look up, believer, to Jesus now. Let the eye of your faith behold Him with many crowns on His head. Remember that you will one day be like Him, when you will see Him as He is. You will not be as great as He is; you will not be as divine, but still you will, in a measure, share the same honors and enjoy the same happiness and the same dignity that He possesses. Be content to live unknown for a little while and to walk your weary way through the fields of poverty or up the hills of affliction. Soon you will reign with Christ, for He has *"made us kings and priests unto God"* (Rev. 1:6), and we will reign with Him forever and ever. Oh, wonderful thought for the children of God! We have Christ for our glorious representative in heaven's courts now, and soon He will come and receive us to Himself to be with Him there, to behold His glory, and to share His joy.

```
F  R  T  I  E  H  R  E  X  A  L  T  A  T  I  O  N  E  M  U
I  A  O  U  R  M  G  K  F  P  H  I  H  O  F  A  E  C  R  N
P  R  F  G  R  Z  I  F  T  B  Q  K  F  R  G  X  O  I  S  D
X  R  T  F  V  Z  W  N  H  Q  U  E  G  I  O  Y  C  Z  A  I
G  F  A  L  O  U  H  C  E  E  S  S  V  S  N  N  L  O  I  S
I  R  P  A  O  R  R  C  E  N  R  N  O  A  Z  I  E  H  N  P
G  E  J  H  X  G  D  Z  P  R  T  I  O  B  H  Z  T  M  T  U
M  P  L  S  W  T  R  S  W  E  P  D  T  Q  R  C  Z  E  S  T
E  R  E  B  N  V  J  E  Q  M  E  E  E  A  O  I  S  H  J  E
D  E  C  R  K  E  D  W  F  E  B  A  T  W  G  N  D  D  H  D
I  S  Z  I  Q  C  L  Y  I  M  N  D  P  Q  W  E  L  E  B  F
A  E  B  B  X  F  H  G  J  B  F  Y  Q  H  K  H  K  H  J  H
T  N  W  M  Z  T  L  L  N  E  A  J  U  R  Z  F  I  N  K  H
O  T  M  V  N  Q  I  N  V  R  Z  I  V  M  O  P  H  I  R  I
R  A  B  F  B  U  R  I  E  D  Z  S  R  E  O  D  V  P  G  G
C  T  L  S  H  J  B  O  V  X  C  Q  U  E  E  N  K  H  A  H
S  I  V  C  J  V  Y  E  L  D  E  J  H  Y  R  I  G  H  T  E
D  V  C  J  B  A  A  A  H  G  I  F  O  Z  W  E  Q  X  F  S
N  E  D  I  K  M  J  O  X  S  F  T  A  X  N  W  W  C  K  T
F  E  N  U  I  X  P  L  A  C  E  G  L  O  R  I  E  S  M  M
```

DEAD	BURIED	THRONE	HIGHEST
PLACE	AFFORDS	UNDISPUTED	RIGHT
REMEMBER	REPRESENTATIVE	EXALTATION	EMINENT
GLORIES	FINITE	MEDIATOR	HERITAGE
SAINTS	QUEEN	OPHIR	BRIDE

Evening

Thou shalt not be afraid for the terror by night.
—Psalm 91:5

What is this terror? It may be the cry of fire or the noise of thieves or imagined appearances or the shriek of sudden sickness or death. We live in the world of death and sorrow; therefore, we may look for trouble in the nighttime as well as during the glare of the broiling sun. Nor should this alarm us, for no matter what the terror is, the promise is that the believer will not be afraid. Why should he be fearful? Let us make it more personal: why should we be afraid? God our Father is here, and He will be here all through the lonely hours. He is an almighty Watcher, a sleepless Guardian, a faithful Friend. Nothing can happen without His direction, for even hell itself is under His control. Darkness is not dark to Him. He has promised to be a wall of fire around His people: who can break through such a barrier? Unbelievers may well be afraid, for they have an angry God above them, a guilty conscience within them, and a yawning hell below them. But we who rest in Jesus are saved from all these through rich mercy. If we give way to foolish fear, we will dishonor our profession of faith and lead others to doubt the reality of godliness. We ought to be afraid of being afraid, lest we vex the Holy Spirit by foolish distrust. Down, then, dismal foreboding and groundless apprehension. God has not forgotten to be gracious or shut up His tender mercies. It may be night in the soul, but there does not need to be any terror, for the God of love does not change. Children of light may walk through darkness, but they are not cast away. No, they are enabled to prove their adoption by trusting in their heavenly Father as hypocrites cannot do.

Though the night be dark and dreary,
    Darkness cannot hide from Thee;
Thou art He, who, never weary,
    Watchest where Your people be.

```
D A X D I S T R U S T K G A L A R M B I
A N O I Y A W N I N G B R T Y T K P W M
G G K G X C B U P K S I O K P P T Y R I
S H R I E K E N K V M B U K L U E D Q V
F O R E B O D I N G X A N D J L R U I A
W A L V E X C K I Q T W D I F F R N Q A
B M Y K Y Y F Z G W U W L J G O O D Z X
R D L E K W E Q H V T L E M U O R I E Z
R K P M N I F G T X H M S C I L G S Y O
Z P P P I E B C T V N Q S R L I H M N G
G R A C I O U S I U E P L M T S H A Z B
G F J B Z S L M M W G F D U Y H R L Y R
L U H Q V I B B E U M X B Q W D B M A O
K T L S W E P E J K Y Y S U D D E N R I
K Y D J Y W S B K C H X T X E E Z G E L
B Y A N S B S L E E P L E S S F D L E I
J Q P S T S U N D H X S X D O J X A Q N
G C L C J A X H Y V D U W J T T Y R T G
U L R K N W A P P E A R A N C E S E H D
P A Q X D F R I E N D E I G U K W J O A
```

TERROR	APPEARANCES	SHRIEK	SUDDEN
NIGHTTIME	GLARE	BROILING	SUN
ALARM	SLEEPLESS	FRIEND	GUILTY
YAWNING	VEX	FOOLISH	DISTRUST
DISMAL	FOREBODING	GROUNDLESS	GRACIOUS

Morning

This do in remembrance of me.
—1 Corinthians 11:24

The implication from today's text seems to be that Christians may forget Christ! There could be no need for this loving exhortation if there were not a fearful supposition that our memories might prove treacherous. Nor is this a bare supposition. It is, alas, too well confirmed in our experience, not as a possibility, but as a lamentable fact! It appears almost impossible that those who have been redeemed by the blood of the dying Lamb, who have been loved with an everlasting love by the eternal Son of God, could forget that gracious Savior. But, if startling to the ear, it is, alas, too apparent to the eye to allow us to deny the crime. Forget Him who never forgot us! Forget Him who poured His blood forth for our sins! Forget Him who loved us even to the death! Can it be possible? Yes, it is not only possible, but conscience confesses that it is too sadly a fault with all of us, that we permit Him to be as a wayfaring man tarrying but for a night. He whom we should make the abiding tenant of our memories is but a visitor therein. The Cross, where one would think that memory would linger and inattentiveness would be an unknown intruder, is desecrated by the feet of forgetfulness. Does not your conscience say that this is true? Do you not find yourselves forgetful of Jesus? Some creature steals away your heart, and you are unmindful of Him on whom your affection ought to be set. Some earthly business engrosses your attention when you should fix your eye steadily on the Cross. It is the incessant turmoil of the world and the constant attraction of earthly things that take away the soul from Christ. While memory too well preserves a poisonous weed, it permits the Rose of Sharon to wither. Let us charge ourselves to bind a heavenly forget-me-not about our hearts for Jesus our Beloved, and, whatever else we let slip, let us hold fast to Him.

```
I V W U S F O R G E T F U L N E S S M H
M I J A N T M Y U B Y F B J D I P A C X
P X C C S M A W J X K I T S E T T T S N
L F C H C E I R V T U G Y E D J B T U G
I L O J T T A N T T A K Z A E U I E P M
C A N E E M R D L R Q A A E J H N P Q
A M S H N R A P A F I F X T M U Q T O L
T E C P A N P B E R U N F A E R M I S K
I N I S N A O D I H B L G R D I N O I E
O T E H T L R P D D K T Q R Z Y X N T X
N A N U N K N O W N I T H Y R T I K I H
T B C L G Q B A W N P N V I C E P Z O O
V L E K L K P L Z M O K G N U L I X N R
S E A Y F N I T R V E E X G H M I T K A
P S U P P K H U T R E A C H E R O U S T
L I N A T T E N T I V E N E S S Q N T I
R O M Q K I N T R U D E R Y J C Q T N O
Y D E N U D G Q L J E C D P Y F Y X Y N
P U H U O J J T F E A R F U L S G I X V
R W H X F B M V S W A Y F A R I N G P Z
```

IMPLICATION	EXHORTATION	FEARFUL	SUPPOSITION
TREACHEROUS	LAMENTABLE	REDEEMED	ETERNAL
STARTLING	CONSCIENCE	WAYFARING	TARRYING
ABIDING	TENANT	INATTENTIVENESS	UNKNOWN
INTRUDER	FORGETFULNESS	UNMINDFUL	ATTENTION

Evening

Blessed is he that watcheth.
—Revelation 16:15

I *die daily*" (1 Cor. 15:31), said the apostle Paul. This was the life of the early Christians. They went everywhere with their lives in their hands. In this day, we are not called to pass through the same fearful persecutions. If we were, the Lord would give us grace to bear the test; but the tests of the Christian life, at the present moment, though outwardly not as terrible, are yet more likely to overcome us than even those of the fiery age. If we have to bear the ridicule of the world, that is not so hard. Its flattery, its soft words, its oily speeches, its fawning, and its hypocrisy are far worse. Our danger is that we would grow rich and become proud, that we would give ourselves up to the trends of this present evil world and lose our faith. If wealth is not our trial, worldly care is just as dangerous. If we cannot be torn in pieces by the roaring lion, we may be hugged to death by the bear. The devil does not care which it is, as long as he destroys our love for Christ and our confidence in Him. I fear that the Christian church is far more likely to lose her integrity in these soft and silken days than in those rougher times. We must be awake now, for we travel on enchanted ground, and we are most likely to fall asleep, to our own undoing, unless our faith in Jesus is a reality and our love for Jesus a vehement flame. Many in these days of easy profession are likely to prove to be tares, and not wheat; hypocrites with fair masks on their faces, but not the true-born children of the living God. Christian, do not think that these are times in which you can dispense with watchfulness or with holy ardor. You need these things more than ever, and may God the eternal Spirit display His omnipotence in you so that you may be able to say, in all these softer things, as well as in the rougher, *"We are more than conquerors through him that loved us"* (Rom. 8:37).

```
I  H  Y  P  O  C  R  I  S  Y  N  D  J  H  A  Z  Z  J  S  X
H  N  T  F  E  Z  W  D  J  W  A  P  A  N  A  N  K  N  S  E
F  Z  E  X  L  V  D  F  L  A  M  E  R  I  T  H  Q  S  P  V
A  D  G  G  O  U  T  W  A  R  D  L  Y  O  L  D  C  O  E  K
W  J  A  J  R  J  W  F  L  E  G  H  B  D  U  Y  S  I  E  O
N  C  M  N  I  I  S  I  L  K  E  N  Q  P  A  D  G  R  C  J
I  S  W  C  G  D  T  L  L  S  S  M  P  W  W  W  B  O  H  F
N  L  H  H  O  E  Q  Y  C  A  F  B  I  U  Q  D  H  L  E  E
G  O  Y  Z  C  V  R  N  Q  D  J  G  Z  G  W  J  Z  V  S  Y
T  H  D  D  Z  Q  P  O  A  F  I  E  R  Y  O  H  W  E  I  J
J  P  R  D  R  X  S  N  U  V  F  E  O  C  R  R  T  H  V  G
X  R  I  D  I  C  U  L  E  S  Z  D  K  M  L  O  M  E  E  H
E  T  U  M  H  R  O  U  G  H  E  R  F  C  D  A  C  M  W  W
X  V  Q  R  A  G  T  M  J  F  Y  F  D  G  L  R  S  E  V  S
B  Y  R  R  J  J  R  V  K  H  F  H  O  O  Y  I  F  N  Q  R
S  I  C  P  A  Y  T  W  O  R  P  Y  G  I  W  N  E  T  F  N
T  C  M  E  N  C  H  A  N  T  E  D  O  L  L  G  K  F  T  C
X  T  P  I  M  Y  X  Q  G  C  D  O  M  K  N  Y  K  V  P  D
P  E  R  S  E  C  U  T  I  O  N  S  O  T  R  C  A  V  N  E
H  U  F  L  A  T  T  E  R  Y  J  D  X  F  D  G  U  X  P  U
```

DAILY	PERSECUTIONS	OUTWARDLY	FIERY
RIDICULE	FLATTERY	OILY	SPEECHES
FAWNING	HYPOCRISY	PROUD	WORLDLY
DANGEROUS	ROARING	INTEGRITY	SILKEN
ROUGHER	ENCHANTED	VEHEMENT	FLAME

Morning

I pray not that thou shouldest take them out of the world.
—John 17:15

A sweet and blessed event that will occur to all believers in God's own time is the going home to be with Jesus. In a few more years the Lord's soldiers, who are now fighting *"the good fight of faith"* (1 Tim. 6:12), will be finished with conflict and will have entered into the joy of their Lord. But although Christ prays that His people may eventually be with Him where He is, He does not ask that they may be taken at once away from this world to heaven. He wishes them to stay here. Yet how frequently does the wearied pilgrim offer up the prayer, *"Oh that I had wings like a dove! for then would I fly away, and be at rest"* (Ps. 55:6), but Christ does not pray like that. He leaves us in His Father's hands, until, like shocks of fully ripened corn, we will each be gathered into our Master's granary. Jesus does not plead for our instant removal by death, for to abide in the flesh is necessary for others if not profitable for ourselves. He asks that we may be kept from evil, but He never asks for us to be admitted to the inheritance in glory until we are of full age. Christians often want to die when they have any trouble. Ask them why, and they tell you, "Because we would be with the Lord." We fear it is not so much that they are longing to be with the Lord, but rather that they are desiring to get rid of their troubles; otherwise, they would feel the same wish to die at other times, when not under the pressure of trial. They want to go home, not so much for the Savior's company, as to be at rest. Now it is quite right to desire to depart if we can do it in the same spirit that Paul did, because to be with Christ is far better, but the wish to escape from trouble is a selfish one. Rather let your care and wish be to glorify God by your life here as long as He pleases, even though it is in the midst of toil, conflict, and suffering, and leave it to Him to say when it is enough.

```
T F R E Q U E N T L Y C Y P D Y W G S J
W R F I C K E Y V T X I X I E E L J O U
G B Q E P O C C X W L D W L C V M W S J
M F B L L E M Q O C C U R G Q O A E C B
B I H E O F N U B V R Q U R N P J A O E
Z G B V Q D L E E N U V G I I R L R R L
L H B E O V T A D B Z A M J M V I N I
V T P N O D S O L D I E R S L Y E E G E
K I V T G M H Q J Z K C C M X B N D Y V
X N M U M Q C V S H O C K S N U G E U E
B G H A Y G X I H C Q C E V E N T J B R
H M P L J G Q Z A G E C T T R U B X I S
E L O L V G L O H O T H E R W I S E N F
D S V Y P R O F I T A B L E D V Z O S S
B L E S S E D G R N S L O N G I N G T W
T R O U B L E S S C K J D W A U Z A A E
B S H N J J J L B Y P P M Q G C U A N E
V V R L X V A B M S B D N U Y V L U T T
R H O M E J F T N D K T V S Z Q V A V U
Y I M N E K S G G O O H Q M J M O O Q M
```

SWEET	BLESSED	EVENT	OCCUR
BELIEVERS	HOME	SOLDIERS	FIGHTING
EVENTUALLY	FREQUENTLY	WEARIED	PILGRIM
SHOCKS	RIPENED	CORN	INSTANT
PROFITABLE	LONGING	TROUBLES	OTHERWISE

These all died in faith.
—Hebrews 11:13

Behold the epitaph of all those blessed saints who passed away before the coming of our Lord! It does not matter how they died, whether of old age or by violent means. This one point in which they all agree is the worthiest to record: *"These all died in faith."* In faith they lived. It was their comfort, their guide, their motive, and their support; and, in the same spiritual grace, they died, ending their life-song in the sweet strain in which they had so long continued. They did not die resting in the flesh or on their own achievements. They never wavered from their first acceptance of God's will, but they held to the way of faith to the end. Faith is as precious to die by as to live by. Dying in faith has distinct reference to the past. They believed the promises that had gone before and were assured that their sins were blotted out through the mercy of God. Dying in faith has to do with the present. These saints were confident of their acceptance with God. They enjoyed the rays of His love and rested in His faithfulness. Dying in faith looks into the future. They fell *"asleep in Christ"* (1 Cor. 15:18), affirming that the Messiah would surely come, and that when He would in the last days appear on the earth, they would rise from their graves to behold Him. To them the pains of death were but the birth pangs of a better state. Take courage, my soul, as you read this epitaph. Your life's journey is one of faith through grace, and sight seldom cheers you; this has also been the pathway of the brightest and the best. Faith was the orbit in which these stars of the first magnitude moved during all the time of their shining here; you will be happy if that it is also your path. Look anew tonight to Jesus, the Author and Finisher of your faith, and thank Him for giving you the same precious faith that belonged to the souls who are now in glory.

```
B L C P A U U Q M A G N I T U D E S B X
L K M D S S S J J C W I C D D F B S P V
O X W N S B P A N G S M N J K E H J R W
T B L W U R P W V E Z X E E M S T Q R O
T I K E R P G K R L S O M I S Y U V E R
E D S F E J Y S G M S G O U T X A I C T
D P T F D E E T T G P C T N K M F U O H
D D R J L J S X J B I V I V U A F R R I
C L A W B E Q Q B Q R U V W O Y I G D E
I W I N Y E S Y F Q I Y E U V B R R L S
V Z N N H E H H O E T V K O T T M A H T
R E T T X T R O Y W U E Y C S G I V P B
O C P V X L W E L B A H L R B C N E A K
V S U I L T O S S D L S L T H Z G S S I
Q H J Y C S K W T B V L G V U Z P S Y
C O Y O U A U Q F N I K N D G G L W E V
C C C P Q Z P O A R E N O W K N J H D Z
W G A W A Y B H R S G M G Y O Y Q N N G
V I O L E N T Z I E W M W A V E R E D I
B M S M E A N S I H W Q P D A E T B W C
```

BEHOLD	EPITAPH	PASSED	AWAY
VIOLENT	MEANS	WORTHIEST	RECORD
MOTIVE	SPIRITUAL	STRAIN	RESTING
FLESH	WAVERED	ASSURED	BLOTTED
AFFIRMING	GRAVES	PANGS	MAGNITUDE

Morning

Who hath blessed us with all spiritual blessings.
—Ephesians 1:3

Christ bestows on His people all the goodness of the past, present, and the future. In the mysterious ages of the past, the Lord Jesus was His Father's first elect. In His election He gave us an interest, for we were *chosen…in him before the foundation of the world*" (Eph. 1:4). He had from all eternity the privileges of Sonship, as His Father's Only Begotten and well-beloved Son. He has, in the riches of His grace, by adoption and regeneration, elevated us to sonship also, so that to us He has given *"power to become the sons of God"* (John 1:12). The eternal covenant, based on suretyship and confirmed by oath, is ours, for our strong consolation and security. In the everlasting settlements of predestinating wisdom and omnipotent decree, the eyes of the Lord Jesus were ever fixed on us. We may rest assured that in the whole roll of destiny there is not a line that lessens the interests of His redeemed. The great betrothal of the Prince of Glory is ours, for it is to us that He is betrothed, as the sacred nuptials will before long declare to an assembled universe. The marvelous incarnation of the God of heaven, with all the amazing condescension and humiliation that attended it, is ours. The bloody sweat, the scourge, and the cross are ours forever. Whatever blissful consequences flow from perfect obedience, finished atonement, resurrection, ascension, or intercession—all are ours by His own gift. He is now bearing our names on His breastplate; and in His authoritative pleadings at the throne, He remembers our persons and pleads our cause. He employs His dominion over principalities and powers and His absolute majesty in heaven for the benefit of those who trust in Him. His high estate is as much at our service as was His condition of abasement. He who gave Himself for us in the depths of woe and death does not withdraw the grant now that He is enthroned in the highest heavens.

```
R Z A W W C E V A G E S O N S H I P L S
B O F C X Y I T K E S X M P U Y N K B V
N U P T I A L S E S T I H J V M T H E A
Z R V A Z B U D W R B J E O P Y E I T Y
Y W N Z B Z U E I A N D E K X S R I R D
Y B Y G E C B H Y X T I Q P P T E R O I
D Z P E S K R I R C V J T V W E S R T B
Y H L V T R E J R A G Q O Y X R T M H W
A H S Y O S P M W Z W V K A Y I K K A T
Q R W H W M G O O D N E S S W O U O L F
C X R U S Q C O V E N A N T C U Q Q S E
Z F S P P S U R E T Y S H I P S Q G O L
X I A D O P T I O N Z I C A U H D Z E E
I Z S A E F D P G I W M P F J X F Q V V
R J Y O U L U A A T W W M E F I X E D A
Y T M A O X G T U S S K F B S L N Z O T
E L E C T I O N U I T U P R E S E N T E
A X K Q N E N S Y R Z G O J Y N Z A H D
U P R I N C E R M G E Q V F H Q Y T C C
V P R E G E N E R A T I O N G Z K E Q P
```

BESTOWS	GOODNESS	PAST	PRESENT
FUTURE	MYSTERIOUS	AGES	ELECTION
INTEREST	ETERNITY	SONSHIP	ADOPTION
REGENERATION	ELEVATED	COVENANT	SURETYSHIP
FIXED	BETROTHAL	PRINCE	NUPTIALS

77

Evening

*Come, my beloved, let us go forth into the field;...
let us see if the vine flourish.*
—Song of Solomon 7:11–12

The church was about to engage in earnest labor and desired her Lord's company in it. She did not say, "I will go," but *"Let us go."* It is a blessing to work when Jesus is at our side! It is the business of God's people to be trimmers of God's vines. Like our first parents, we are put into the garden of the Lord for usefulness; therefore, let us go forth into the field. Observe that the church, when she is thinking rightly, desires to enjoy communion with Christ in all her many labors. Some imagine that they cannot serve Christ actively and still have fellowship with Him. They are mistaken. True, it is very easy to fritter away our inward life in outward activities and complain to the Spouse, *"They made me the keeper of the vineyards; but mine own vineyard have I not kept"* (Song 1:6). There is no reason, however, why this should be the case except through our own folly and neglect. Certainly, a believer may do nothing, yet grow quite as lifeless in spiritual things as those who are the busiest. Mary was not praised for sitting still, but for sitting at Jesus' feet. Even so, Christians are not to be praised for neglecting duties under the pretense of having secret fellowship with Jesus. It is not sitting, but sitting at Jesus' feet that is commendable. Do not think that activity is in itself evil. It is a great blessing and a means of grace to us. Paul called it a grace given to him to be allowed to preach, and every form of Christian service may become a personal blessing to those engaged in it. Those who have the most fellowship with Christ are not recluses or hermits, who have much time to spare, but indefatigable laborers who are toiling for Jesus, and who, in their labors, have Him side by side with them, so that they are *"workers together"* (2 Cor. 6:1) with God. Let us remember that in anything we have to do for Jesus, we can do it and should do it in close communion with Him.

```
M L N N Q J N K P H M J G X E U D L X C
M I I W K T G V H R T Y P P A U U U J Q
P U S R K O M Z Z G E Q F Y K R C S F U
V B S T Y A K A X W S T L O S O U E B V
I F E G A C P L R G E I E L L U Q F R T
P W C T Y K Y W Q S B H N B L Q U A X
I E R C R Z E R F I C O Z S S N Y L B B
T Z E R E I E N B L J Q G U T E A N S H
N K T H I R M L I A U V J N R T S E I P
E L Y U H U T M B B B F I E E G E S A P
G P O Z M T P A E O O I N N S E I S E A
L C D O W U E F I R E G R G E M N P A R
E V J R I F E E A N S V A A V S W J R E
C S B N Q C I B U M L B U G R E A O N N
T T W C Y H J G T J E Y U E R S R X E T
Z I C M M V M L O O I X N F E O D B S S
K L K H M X F C G M B U S I N E S S T N
Z L G Z L S Q R I G H T L Y L A E N H A
F R I T T E R P Y L T T G C J I F C B D
R F Q E A C T I V E L Y A W N C E L R S
```

ENGAGE   EARNEST   LABOR   BUSINESS
TRIMMERS   VINES   PARENTS   USEFULNESS
RIGHTLY   ACTIVELY   MISTAKEN   FRITTER
INWARD   FOLLY   NEGLECT   CERTAINLY
MARY   STILL   PRETENSE   SECRET

Morning

Who giveth us richly all things to enjoy.
—1 Timothy 6:17

Our Lord Jesus is always giving. Not for a solitary instant does He withdraw His hand. As long as there is a vessel of grace not yet full to the brim, the oil will not be withheld. He is a sun that always shines. He is manna always falling round the camp. He is a rock in the desert that ever sends out streams of life from His smitten side. The rain of His grace is always falling; the river of His bounty is always flowing, and the wellspring of His love is constantly overflowing. As the King can never die, so His grace can never fail. Daily we pluck His fruit, and daily His branches bend down to our hand with a fresh store of mercy. There are seven feast days in His weeks, and as many as are the days, so many are the banquets in His years. Who has ever returned from His door unblessed? Who has ever risen from His table unsatisfied, or from His heart unloved? His mercies are *"new every morning"* (Lam. 3:23) and fresh every evening. Who can know the number of His benefits or recount the list of His bounties? Every grain of sand that drops from the glass of time is but the tardy follower of a myriad of mercies. The wings of our hours are covered with the silver of His kindness and with the gold of His affection. The river of time bears from the mountains of eternity the golden sands of His favor. The countless stars are but as the standard bearers of a more innumerable host of blessings. *"Who can count the dust of Jacob, and the number of the fourth part of Israel?"* (Num. 23:10). How will my soul extol Him *"who daily loadeth us with benefits"* (Ps. 68:19), and *"who crowneth [us] with lovingkindness"* (Ps. 103:4)? Oh, that my praise could be as ceaseless as His bounty! O miserable tongue, how can you be silent? Wake up, I pray you, lest I call you no more my glory, but my shame. *"Awake, psaltery and harp: I myself will awake early"* (Ps. 108:2).

```
V O W U F A D C E A S E L E S S U Q V R
A W O L M A N N A V J B N R L W O S P B
H N V O X A L U O P B P M H M B I J O O
S D E V I K X W I T H D R A W K L A L U
U H V I Q S K H G A S T E D V G N C C N
H K N N Z V R V E S S E L Z E L E O A T
G M C G B P Y A O E L X R G U E B B M Y
S Y T K N C W K E N G L H I T F G S P P
B S M I T T E N P L P F I V Z J L K J Y
S Y N N M S N B O Y T V I I N L H B B F
Z Y B D J Z J L F R W S J N S Z O N K A
E E P N D L S Z L F P Q F G H Y P P Z L
K K L E K W K P E Y W S X Z K W E G J L
U H U S O X Y C L Y W F A R A X G A Q I
L B C S K U J L D X R M O L D S W X P N
C K K N S B S O L I T A R Y T U N T A G
Z E M G B R I M N J L E J J F E W Y R X
B R A N C H E S Q A S K E P S R R Y N Q
W K O V E R F L O W I N G K G V H Y L W
R W E L L S P R I N G F M M U G X D N V
```

GIVING	SOLITARY	WITHDRAW	VESSEL
BRIM	OIL	MANNA	FALLING
CAMP	SMITTEN	BOUNTY	WELLSPRING
OVERFLOWING	PLUCK	BRANCHES	JACOB
ISRAEL	LOVINGKINDNESS	CEASELESS	PSALTERY

Evening

*And he said, Thus saith the L*ORD*, Make this valley full of ditches. For thus saith the*
L*ORD*, *Ye shall not see wind, neither shall ye see rain; yet that valley shall be filled*
with water, that ye may drink, both ye, and your cattle, and your beasts.
—2 Kings 3:16–17

The armies of the three kings were famishing from a lack of water. God was about to send it, and in these words the prophet announced the coming blessing. Here was a case of human helplessness. All the valiant men could not procure a drop of water from the skies or find any in the wells of earth. In the same way, the people of the Lord are often at their wits' end; they see their own inadequacy and discover where their help is to be found. Still the people were to prepare by faith for the divine blessing; they were to dig the trenches in which the precious liquid would be held. The church must by her varied agencies, efforts, and prayers make herself ready to be blessed; she must make the pools, and the Lord will fill them. This must be done in faith, in the full assurance that the blessing is about to descend. Soon there was a wonderful bestowal of the needed blessing. The shower did not pour from the clouds as it did in Elijah's case, but, in a silent and mysterious manner, the pools were filled. The Lord has His own sovereign methods of action. He is not tied to manner and time as we are, but He does as He pleases among the sons of men. It is ours to receive from Him thankfully and not to dictate to Him. We must also notice the remarkable abundance of the supply: there was enough to meet everyone's needs. And so it is in the gospel blessing. All the needs of the congregation and of the entire church will be met by divine power in answer to prayer; above all this, victory will be speedily given to the armies of the Lord. What am I doing for Jesus? What trenches am I digging? O Lord, make me ready to receive the blessing that You are so willing to bestow.

```
Z Z H D E S C E N D Q C A R M I E S E L
D I C T A T E N B G L O D N W W S C I W
A I K P O G V S L R Y S B E T T I I K V
L N A G E N C I E S V J U G G Z D T Z K
C S O X Y G V W L K V N Z L P T S A S I
X D T Z T E C L Y N A V Z F P Q Y Y K N
W O F A B U N D A N C E R L R R L Z Q G
A Y X U C Q X W I X K S E H O Q I L W S
A S S U R A N C E D G O M E C P M Z I D
Z Z F A M I S H I N G V A L U U L R W C
Q P E R P V C E H G W E R P R W C Y S O
Z U E M M Q W L P V O R K L E I I I G M
D I G G I N G U K Y H E A E H O V Y A I
Z M V A L I A N T O Q I B S Y Y Q W X N
F V T Y Q S T Y D X J G L S I V U A G G
A N N O U N C E D C E N E N J B D U X P
R T F C Y Z C B G D K T R E N C H E S X
J K B F M E L K I H B L A S M H A G J Q
K O A I N A D E Q U A C Y S M U E J O J
J Y D W X C O N G R E G A T I O N E W X
```

ARMIES	KINGS	FAMISHING	ANNOUNCED
COMING	HELPLESSNESS	VALIANT	PROCURE
WITS	INADEQUACY	TRENCHES	AGENCIES
ASSURANCE	DESCEND	SOVEREIGN	DICTATE
REMARKABLE	ABUNDANCE	CONGREGATION	DIGGING

Morning

*So Mephibosheth dwelt in Jerusalem: for he did eat continually
at the king's table; and was lame on both his feet.*
—2 Samuel 9:13

Mephibosheth was no great ornament to a royal table, yet he had a continual place at David's board, because the king could see in his face the features of the beloved Jonathan. Like Mephibosheth, we may cry unto the King of Glory, *"What is thy servant, that thou shouldest look upon such a dead dog as I am?"* (2 Sam. 9:8). But still, the Lord indulges us with most familiar communion with Himself, because He sees in our countenances the remembrance of His dearly beloved Jesus. The Lord's people are dear for Another's sake. Such is the love that the Father bears for His Only Begotten that for His sake He raises His lowly brethren from poverty and banishment to courtly companionship, noble rank, and royal provision. Their deformity will not rob them of their privileges. Lameness is no bar to sonship; the cripple is as much the heir as if he could run like Asahel, who *"was as light of foot as a wild roe"* (2 Sam. 2:18). Our right does not limp, though our might may. A king's table is a noble hiding place for lame legs, and at the gospel feast we learn to glory in infirmities, because the power of Christ rests on us. Yet grievous disability may mar the persons of the best-loved saints. Here is one feasted by David, and yet so lame in both his feet that he could not go up with the king when he fled from the city, and was therefore maligned and injured by his servant Ziba. Saints whose faith is weak, and whose knowledge is slender, are great losers; they are exposed to many enemies and cannot follow the king wherever he goes. This disease frequently arises from falls. Bad nursing in their spiritual infancy often causes converts to fall into a despondency from which they never recover, and sin in other cases brings broken bones. Lord, help the lame to leap like a deer and satisfy all Your people with the bread of Your table!

```
G P O V E R T Y C X L R U I I H U S D Y
B L P T I A D F M Q B E G O T T E N E T
D E F O R M I T Y O V L H W R Y W L S L
C O N T I N U A L H Z I N H O C Z E P I
G N O B L E K J A C N G Q R X L J N O M
B U C E Z D B J F Z L O W L Y P E Q N E
B A N I S H M E N T H I Z M M G C P D P
Q N I N D U L G E S J O E P F L C C E H
X R O R N A M E N T W Q S V L Q O Z N I
C V P I C W D Y C I A B A N B K U L C B
W I D O V A B N Y O S O K X L N R W Y O
F P Q N C H J V W Y Q A E L R W T C M S
W P T G L R L F P G I R B H A J L O N H
E K F V X T T Q Y N K D E J S C Y I U E
B W L A M E N E S S W N Y M A Q Q M R T
Y V F C R G X V N P X H R P H X Y C S H
K K C Z E C W I B F J S L A E N C S I O
J O N A T H A N W X X J V H L C F R N D
B C R M B N O L O J G X K A Q R O O G Y
Z I B A C H H V M C C R I P P L E Q P E
```

MEPHIBOSHETH	ORNAMENT	CONTINUAL	BOARD
JONATHAN	INDULGES	BEGOTTEN	SAKE
LOWLY	POVERTY	BANISHMENT	COURTLY
NOBLE	DEFORMITY	LAMENESS	CRIPPLE
ASAHEL	ZIBA	NURSING	DESPONDENCY

Evening

What is thy servant, that thou shouldest look upon
such a dead dog as I am?
—2 Samuel 9:8

If Mephibosheth was thus humbled by David's kindness, what will we be in the presence of our gracious Lord? The more grace we have, the less we will think of ourselves, for grace, like light, reveals our impurity. Eminent saints have scarcely known to what to compare themselves; their sense of unworthiness has been so clear and keen. "I am," said holy Rutherford, "a dry and withered branch, a piece of dead carcass, dry bones, and not able to step over a straw." In another place he wrote, "Except as to open outbreakings, I want nothing of what Judas and Cain had." The lowliest objects in nature appear to the humbled mind to have a preference above itself, because they have never contracted sin. A dog may be greedy, fierce, or filthy, but it has no conscience to violate, no Holy Spirit to resist. A dog may be a worthless animal, yet by a little kindness, it is soon won to love its master and is faithful to death. But we forget the goodness of the Lord and do not respond to His call. The term *"dead dog"* is the most expressive of all terms of contempt, but it is not too strong to use to express the self-abhorrence of instructed believers. They do not pretend to be modest; they mean what they say. They have weighed themselves in the balances of the sanctuary and realized the vanity of their natures. At best, we are but clay, animated dust, mere walking hills; but viewed as sinners, we are monsters indeed. Let it be published in heaven as a miracle that the Lord Jesus would set His heart's love upon such as we. Dust and ashes though we are, we must and will magnify the *"exceeding greatness of his power"* (Eph. 1:19). Could not His heart find rest in heaven? Must He come to these tents of Kedar for a spouse and choose a bride on whom the sun had looked? (See Song of Solomon 1:5–6.) O heavens and earth, break forth into song, and give all glory to our sweet Lord Jesus.

```
E N Y S Y S H Q R Z G R Y R E E M A I R
L I M C B L I X C G V H I Y X A O A R U
D T O A P M A N G H N Y Y W C K U S V G
U E N R G S T U N J I F D Z F B R H T J
S K S C A G W Q A L N Z V M M Z S E G A
T M T E Y P R E S E N C E H F E E S P N
E G E L O W L I E S T R G F L U L M M I
A C R Y U N W O R T H I N E S S V C D M
T N S G R E E D Y Z B W M H C N E V T A
J U N D Z Z F X Y W T Q G P H R S R W T
E M Z W K K I O W C Z A W Y U L K R Y E
Y D P B V S P X I O B H S E Y R H A V D
J E U Q I B O M T N N R B T V L I H K F
V A C A J I N X H T W J V E Z Y W T W I
Q H U M B L E D E E A S T R A W L E Y E
B M G M B W P G R M S H S V K R P X N R
G D N W K E E N E P Z X J V N Z H M B C
W J K K V W S X D T R C A R C A S S H E
G N E X P R E S S I V E N M D Z A K N M
V N B X R U T H E R F O R D S F N A G W
```

HUMBLED	PRESENCE	OURSELVES	IMPURITY
SCARCELY	UNWORTHINESS	KEEN	RUTHERFORD
WITHERED	CARCASS	STRAW	LOWLIEST
GREEDY	FIERCE	EXPRESSIVE	CONTEMPT
ANIMATED	MONSTERS	DUST	ASHES

Morning

These were the potters, and those that dwelt among plants and hedges:
there they dwelt with the king for his work.
—1 Chronicles 4:23

Potters were the very highest grade of workers, but the king needed potters; therefore, they were in royal service, although the material on which they worked was nothing but clay. We, too, may be engaged in the most menial part of the Lord's work, but it is a great privilege to do anything for our King; therefore, we will abide in our calling, hoping that, although we *"have lien among the pots, yet shall [we] be as the wings of a dove covered with silver, and her feathers with yellow gold"* (Ps. 68:13). The text tells us of those who *"dwelt among plants and hedges,"* having rough, rustic hedging and ditching work to do. They may have desired to live in the city, amid its life, society, and refinement, but they kept their appointed places, for they were doing the king's work. The place of our habitation is fixed, and we are not to leave it out of whim and caprice, but seek to serve the Lord in it, by being a blessing to those among whom we reside. These potters and gardeners had royal company, for *"they dwelt with the king."* Although they lived among hedges and plants, they dwelt with the king there. No lawful place or gracious occupation, however lowly, can exclude us from communion with our divine Lord. In visiting hovels, crowded rooming houses, workhouses, or jails, we may go with the King. In all works of faith we may count on Jesus' fellowship. It is when we are in His work that we may depend on His smile. You unknown workers who are occupied for your Lord amid the dirt and wretchedness of the lowest of the low, be of good cheer, for jewels have been found on dunghills before now, earthen pots have been filled with heavenly treasure, and bad weeds have been transformed into precious flowers. Dwell with the King for His work, and when He writes His chronicles, your name will be recorded.

```
C G D R S T L Y G W O P G O Z W Z W V N
H B A O X Y B P T B X C R C Y Y U R W Y
M L U X V J Z D Z H Y Z A T A Y S E R U
T Z M I M E L C B A E B D C Q J O T E T
C X Q G A W T A Q R U R E J I Q C C F W
Q A D V G S U L J S X T E F F K I H I I
O E Y Q S Z K L H O I J B F A L E E N N
F G H W V F S I W M B Z H M O O T D E G
O E R P T H J N H J O R S X L R Y N M S
M G A O L W Z G X Z O C V R Z Q E E E U
D D J T V R M E N I A L V O H O O S N F
S N S T H O M B N M W W R Y L Z Q S T P
E I K E H E D G E S Z H Y A U R O V J Y
R D V R W T R I M U S S P L M S T F L S
V J Q S U U U S D I T C H I N G Z J I C
I L D H C L A Y J G R L A P F F F L E E
C B N D B R U S T I C Z J B D Q Y I N X
E M O X R W Z Q I O U S N O I F W U V F
K O I E K C A P R I C E Q L F Y C J W L
E R B A X Q K B U T X T D G W H I M P Z
```

GRADE	POTTERS	THEREFORE	ROYAL
SERVICE	CLAY	MENIAL	CALLING
LIEN	WINGS	DOVE	FEATHERS
HEDGES	RUSTIC	DITCHING	SOCIETY
REFINEMENT	WHIM	CAPRICE	WRETCHEDNESS

Evening

He humbled himself.
—Philippians 2:8

Jesus is the great Teacher of true humility. Daily we need to learn of Him. See the Master taking a towel and washing His disciples' feet! Follower of Christ, will you not humble yourself? See Him as the Servant of servants, and surely you cannot be proud! Is not this sentence the summary of His biography: *"He humbled himself"*? While on earth, was He not always stripping off first one robe of honor and then another, until, naked, He was nailed to the cross? Did He not empty His inmost self, pouring out His lifeblood, giving up all for us, until they laid Him penniless in a borrowed grave? How low was our dear Redeemer brought! How then can we be proud? Stand at the foot of the cross, and count the purple drops by which you have been cleansed. Wear the crown of thorns. Observe His scourged shoulders, still gushing with the crimson stream of His blood. See His hands and feet given up to the rough iron, and His whole self to mockery and scorn. Notice the bitterness, the anguish, and the pain of inward grief showing themselves in His outward frame. Hear the chilling cry, *"My God, my God, why hast thou forsaken me?"* (Matt. 27:46). And if you do not lie prostrate on the ground before that cross, you have never seen it. If you are not humbled in the presence of Jesus, you do not know Him. You were so lost that nothing could save you but the sacrifice of God's only begotten Son. Think of that, and as Jesus stooped for you, bow yourself in lowliness at His feet. A sense of Christ's amazing love for us has a greater tendency to humble us than even a consciousness of our own guilt. May the Lord bring us in contemplation to Calvary. Then our position will no longer be that of a pompous man of pride, but we will assume the humble place of one who loves much because he has had much forgiven. Pride cannot live beneath the cross. Let us sit there and learn our lesson, and then rise and put it into practice.

S H S D M H S J C P J B Q Q D O C R T H
H Y T O W O J X I D R I A S J Y O P X P
O C I Z K Y C T U D M O R Y I K O P S E
U H S F Y U W K S S J G G F Y O V U L N
L A B T O K O T E E R R V K N V U R G N
D I O O R F S T H R C A J Z Y A R P Q I
E D F T Z E Z W K Y Y P F E D U O L U L
R D K E M Y A F S U P H L G C B B E K E
S I Z X B V C M O C M Y V L R F E O X S
R S W D Q L Y R O F O N G V O S V G X S
E C S P D M O L I N I U M C S B G M E B
W R P B X O B O P M E K R G S R T C L Z
D O V J L O S G D J S B C G L S L H G D
T W W F T Q F E E T A O E U E S V I U T
V N E F H O N O R D M I N E Q D A L S H
R P Y T R X W S A C S T B V F Q Z L H O
F G P C H P U E H L F H Q K W K W I I R
Y E C Z H U M I L I T Y Z P Q L G N N N
F X P C W B S O I I N M O S T D Q G G S
W D M H O P V B P X O D U I T G C U V E

HUMILITY	TOWEL	FEET	BIOGRAPHY
ROBE	HONOR	CROSS	INMOST
LIFEBLOOD	PENNILESS	PURPLE	CROWN
THORNS	SCOURGED	SHOULDERS	GUSHING
CRIMSON	STREAM	MOCKERY	CHILLING

Morning

We live unto the Lord.
—Romans 14:8

If God had willed it, each of us might have entered heaven at the moment of conversion. It was not absolutely necessary for our preparation for immortality that we should tarry here. It is possible for a person to be taken to heaven and to be found ready to be a partaker of the inheritance of the saints in light, though he has but just believed in Jesus. It is true that our sanctification is a long, continual process, and we will not be perfected until we lay aside our bodies and enter within the veil; but nevertheless, had the Lord so willed it, He might have changed us from imperfection to perfection, and have taken us to heaven at once. Why, then, are we here? Would God keep His children out of paradise a single moment longer than was necessary? Why is the army of the living God still on the battlefield when one charge might give them the victory? Why are His children still wandering here and there through a maze, when a solitary word from His lips would bring them into the center of their hopes in heaven? The answer is—they are here that they may *"live unto the Lord,"* and may bring others to know His love. We remain on earth as sowers to scatter good seed; as ploughmen to break up the fallow ground; as heralds publishing salvation. We are here as the *"salt of the earth"* (Matt. 5:13), to be a blessing to the world. We are here to glorify Christ in our daily lives. We are here as workers for Him, and as *"workers together with him"* (2 Cor. 6:1). Let us see that our lives answer their end. Let us live earnest, useful, holy lives, *"to the praise of the glory of his grace"* (Eph. 1:6). Meanwhile, we long to be with Him and daily sing,

> My heart is with Him on His throne,
> And ill can brook delay;
> Each moment listening for the voice,
> "Rise up, and come away."

```
W Y E N T E R E D H H V U F L B E V T N
S P D Z L F X K B J I P J U N X I H S E
A A T S V I Q M Y L D E A E W I H T X C
N R N K Q J G C A H E R I O P F T S O E
F T C C X M G H B I P P W T K X E W C S
E A U Z T Y I U T B Z A G H Q A T B Z S
U K P B J I D U H X O R X L O N G E R A
N E J R X P F D E I T A P A O Z W H C R
I R R O O R H I Z P J T M D Z D P N I Y
M Q Y O J C R J C Z E I L S I N G L E A
M B C K N Q E O R A B O K P H C D E S P
O W M J Z B D S B Y T N E H N R E P P Y
R B V M R M L J S E D I R I B J L S A M
T H C O E W T F M F F W O K E Z A W R P
A A V M D V T R U E X I O N M I Y I A C
L P A E T A K E N X T G U J G G Q L D W
I E J N L L P A C B E L I E V E D L I T
T D L T G B A T T L E F I E L D D E S A
Y X H D B O O N R C X I M A M Y O D E K
I O J S P O I P L O U G H M E N H P O W
```

WILLED	ENTERED	NECESSARY	PREPARATION
IMMORTALITY	TAKEN	PARTAKER	LIGHT
BELIEVED	TRUE	SANCTIFICATION	PROCESS
PARADISE	SINGLE	MOMENT	LONGER
BATTLEFIELD	PLOUGHMEN	BROOK	DELAY

93

Evening

They are they which testify of me.
—John 5:39

Jesus Christ is the Alpha and Omega of the Bible. He is the constant theme of its sacred pages; from first to last they testify of Him. At the creation we at once discern Him as one of the sacred Trinity. We catch a glimpse of Him in the promise of the woman's Seed. We see Him typified in the ark of Noah. We walk with Abraham, as He sees Messiah's day. We dwell in the tents of Isaac and Jacob, feeding on the gracious promise. We hear the venerable Israel talking of Shiloh, and in the numerous types of the law, we find the Redeemer abundantly foreshadowed. Prophets and kings, priests and preachers, all look one way—they all stand as the cherubs did over the ark, desiring to look within and to read the mystery of God's great propitiation. Even more clearly, in the New Testament, we find our Lord the one pervading subject. It is not an ingot here and there or some gold dust thinly scattered. Here you stand on a solid floor of gold; for the whole substance of the New Testament is Jesus crucified, and even its closing sentence is bejeweled with the Redeemer's name. We should always read Scripture in this light. We should consider the Word to be like a mirror into which Christ looks down from heaven. Then we, looking into it, see His face reflected as in a mirror. It is true that the reflection is dim, but still it is a blessed preparation for seeing Him as we will see Him face-to-face. The Bible contains Jesus Christ's letters to us, perfumed by His love. Its pages are the garments of our King, and they all smell of myrrh, aloes, and cassia. Scripture is the royal chariot in which Jesus rides, and it is paved with love for the daughters of Jerusalem. The Scriptures are the swaddling clothes of the holy child Jesus; unroll them and you find your Savior. The essence of the Word of God is Christ.

```
A C H E R U B S X M O E C S F V U D B C
K R V S P H I F W Y J B D W M M J W X O
V W P H C P R O P I T I A T I O N O H N
E P E I Y D N Y Q I V B N D T E J I I S
T R R L U J I Q Q H K L O E R K E S N T
S M F O G T X S U L E E T F G O I C Z A
G C U H N I E R C K S P C T B Y Q H D N
R A M Z F C T S A E M G J H M I V M C T
C S E Y M O B U T D R W C E D G I Z V Q
X S D M G O P T S I U N N M V O I D N J
N I I G A I N G O T F Y P E E R I G O W
W A D K R S N S D W P Y P F N M G D A O
C N X X M Y D D T G V T B P E V H P H M
N L H I E D F Q K Z C Z J H R K K A Q E
Q H Q P N M V H Y X X Y C W A D O G Z G
D U M F T W E J S P W R A H B C V E E A
E P Q B S C M Z D H N C H U L H Y S C A
W H Y N R A L O E S K M U E E W T A C B
I S A A C Z K D I L Z C L X Z V E N W O
C A L P H A I D R B E J E W E L E D X E
```

ALPHA	OMEGA	BIBLE	CONSTANT
THEME	PAGES	TESTIFY	DISCERN
NOAH	ISAAC	VENERABLE	SHILOH
CHERUBS	PROPITIATION	INGOT	BEJEWELED
PERFUMED	GARMENTS	ALOES	CASSIA

Morning

And they were all filled with the Holy Ghost.
—Acts 2:4

The blessings of this day would be rich if all of us were *"filled with the Holy Ghost."* The consequences of this sacred filling of the soul would be impossible to overestimate. Life, comfort, light, purity, power, peace, and many other precious blessings are inseparable from the Spirit's benign presence. As sacred oil, He anoints the head of the believer, sets him apart to the priesthood of saints, and gives him grace to execute his office aright. As the only truly purifying water, He cleanses us from the power of sin and sanctifies us unto holiness, working in us *"to will and to do of his good pleasure"* (Phil. 2:13). As light, He manifested to us at first our lost estate, and now He reveals the Lord Jesus to us and in us and guides us in the way of righteousness. Enlightened by His pure celestial ray, we are no more darkness but light in the Lord. As fire, He both purges us from dross and sets our consecrated nature on a blaze. He is the sacrificial flame by which we are enabled to offer our whole souls as a *"living sacrifice"* (Rom. 12:1) unto God. As heavenly dew, He removes our barrenness and fertilizes our lives. Oh, that He would drop from above upon us at this early hour! Such morning dew would be a sweet beginning to the day. As the Dove, with wings of peaceful love, He broods over His church and over the souls of believers; and as the Comforter, He dispels the cares and doubts that mar the peace of His beloved. He descends on the chosen as on the Lord in Jordan, and bears witness to their sonship by working in them a filial spirit by which they cry, *"Abba, Father"* (Gal. 4:6). As the wind, He brings the breath of life to men; blowing where He pleases, He performs the quickening operations by which the spiritual creation is animated and sustained. Would to God that we might feel His presence this day and every day.

```
F N W E V O V E R E S T I M A T E Q B P
G D O P X X K Q P X M Y R B G D X D Z R
S Y R W U E A K B C E T Q I E M I H Z I
E T T Q V R C X M K R X I H X N V X C E
S E O H J A I U M Z K T D A Q H I T Q S
T J W S N T G T T W A R A Z P L L G H T
A O B M S R I I Y E M B Q G W B J N N H
T W I M P O S S I B L E N M K V V Y T O
E C E M J N V I F I L L I N G B L W H O
L K A C Q C A S Y Y J L V M A Q P E N D
F R L Z P O W E R Z Z V Q D D T L W Z K
I N S E P A R A B L E G G V A Z I V Z G
P L O C W R E M H A U A H C X K F W P A
A D V D X V C U Z B J O O I F B E V L Z
V W Q F B R E A T H J J S C C Z Z S U V
Z A I H A Q V N H Z B F T H D R O S S H
X T Y A B B A Z S U S T A I N E D W A E
K E P U R I F Y I N G G N H A E C G U L
R R J I H Y I Q B L O W I N G H X U U U
C O N S E Q U E N C E S H H T C Y D D G
```

GHOST   CONSEQUENCES   FILLING   IMPOSSIBLE

OVERESTIMATE   LIFE   PURITY   POWER

INSEPARABLE   BENIGN   PRIESTHOOD   EXECUTE

PURIFYING   WATER   ESTATE   DROSS

ABBA   BREATH   BLOWING   SUSTAINED

Evening

My beloved is mine, and I am his: he feedeth among the lilies. Until the day break, and the shadows flee away, turn, my beloved, and be thou like a roe or a young hart upon the mountains of Bether.
—Song of Solomon 2:16–17

Surely if there is a joyous verse in the Bible it is this: *"My beloved is mine, and I am his."* This thought is so peaceful, so full of assurance, so overrunning with happiness and contentment that it might well have been written by the same hand that penned the Twenty-third Psalm. Although the prospect is exceedingly fair and lovely—earth cannot show its superior—it is not entirely a sunlit landscape. There is a cloud in the sky that casts a shadow over the scene. Listen, *"Until the day break, and the shadows flee away."* There is a word, too, about the *"mountains of Bether,"* or the *"mountains of division,"* and to our love, anything like division is bitterness. Beloved, this may be your present state of mind: you do not doubt your salvation; you know that Christ is yours, but you are not feasting with Him. You understand that you are of vital concern to Him, so that you have no shadow of a doubt of your being His and of His being yours, but still His left hand is not under your head, and His right hand does not embrace you. A shade of sadness is cast over your heart, perhaps by affliction, certainly by the temporary absence of your Lord, so even while exclaiming, *"I am his,"* you are forced to fall to your knees and to pray, *"Until the day break, and the shadows flee away, turn, my beloved."* "Where is He?" asks the soul. And the answer comes, *"He feedeth among the lilies."* If we would find Christ, we must be in communion with His people, and we must come to the ordinances with His saints. Oh, for an evening glimpse of Him! Oh, to dine with Him tonight!

```
E W S P P U V S C E N E U Y K Z Z G P I
N J W Q G G V O J I K U F P Y B T S G C
W E V Y E F J P F R Z N B J F Z Y B P O
R E W L V C H L L M H A P P I N E S S N
I M X I Z C C N T A B Z I M Y M Z S U T
T O G C O V E R R U N N I N G W M U N E
T T H X E Y V T R M D D Y T I W Z P L N
E J K K H E D I C I L V S W K V J E I T
N G F A I R D B C N M Z K C Z L X R T M
K H B N X M B I L E F R A S A L D I W E
D U T V P K N W N V H L J D F P S O M N
J O Y O U S C I K G J S E A Z T E R K T
J N C L U H A I H Q L Z O E X K Z Z C D
B F F I Z M D K J I W Y O S L X B K X B
I F A L T H O U G H Q O W C Q Q I U Q E
H G B I H P E A C E F U L N V E H U Q T
T G E E I Y R U Z E R A C A Z Q U Y D H
G R L S O Z X C D B N D E X D K J L E E
V W Z Y C Z G O B I T T E R N E S S E R
A I X Q P E N N E D O V E R S E B F C A
```

JOYOUS	VERSE	MINE	PEACEFUL
OVERRUNNING	HAPPINESS	CONTENTMENT	WRITTEN
PENNED	ALTHOUGH	EXCEEDINGLY	FAIR
SUPERIOR	SUNLIT	LANDSCAPE	SCENE
FLEE	BETHER	BITTERNESS	LILIES

Morning

Only ye shall not go very far away.
—Exodus 8:28

This is a crafty word from the lips of the arch tyrant Pharaoh. If the poor, enslaved Israelites needed to go out of Egypt, then he bargained with them that it should not be very far away—not too far for them to escape the terror of his arms and the observation of his spies. After the same fashion, the world does not love the lack of conformity of nonconformists or the dissidence of dissenters. It would have us be more charitable and not carry matters with too severe a hand. Death to the world and burial with Christ are experiences that carnal minds treat with ridicule; therefore, the law that sets them forth is almost universally neglected, and even condemned. Worldly wisdom recommends the path of compromise and talks of "moderation." According to this carnal policy, purity is admitted to be very desirable, but we are warned against being too precise; truth is, of course, to be followed, but error is not to be severely denounced. "Yes," says the world, "be spiritually minded by all means, but do not deny yourself a little frivolous society, an occasional ball, and a Christmas visit to a theater. What's the good of crying down a thing when it is so fashionable, and everybody does it?" Multitudes of professors yield to this cunning advice, to their own eternal ruin. If we would follow the Lord wholly, we must go right away into the wilderness of separation and leave the Egypt of the carnal world behind us. We must leave its maxims, its pleasures, and its religion, too, and go far away to the place where the Lord calls His sanctified ones. When the town is on fire, our house cannot be too far from the flames. When the plague is abroad, a man cannot be too far from its haunts. The further from a viper the better, and the further from worldly conformity the better. To all true believers let the trumpet call be sounded, *"Come out from among them, and be ye separate"* (2 Cor. 6:17).

```
X D C C G J G T J A E N S L A V E D A Q
T J O K N P H V A T B E N S C L R X D O
V E N T T A Q Q I Q P R O N I Y C W Y R
B R F H G Z G S O P K M O T H W I M O L
I A O M C Z W E C E E C W A G T O U S W
N I R X J W D S U R J R B Y D X B L H N
B O M G R X V C F S A W C B E C S T K B
P B I T A H O A N A L F Q H F S E I Q P
X A T W A I X P Z G S C T C G J R T A H
D H Y I D K N E K Z F H Z Y F P V U E A
V I E C X Q A E D E V U I T V E A D G R
H B S X S P R Y D V Y W R O N X T E Y A
H W Z S H D A F J E Y A B E N J I S P O
Q J W S I T A J A L X L W F J G O B T H
B A D X P D M F E T M U M H N S N U W V
C R F C T I E T Y R A N T Y Y S L Z R P
P M W G A M E N R D Q D G N R X Z R L O
O S W L I P S S C O T K P L A G U E Q O
N H A U N T S D K E C I G I C I Q Z M R
C V D Z C M B G L G I D D Q H F A Z T O
```

CRAFTY	LIPS	TYRANT	PHARAOH
POOR	ENSLAVED	EGYPT	BARGAINED
ESCAPE	ARMS	OBSERVATION	SPIES
FASHION	CONFORMITY	DISSIDENCE	MULTITUDES
PLAGUE	ABROAD	HAUNTS	VIPER

Evening

Let every man abide in the same calling wherein he was called.
—1 Corinthians 7:20

Some people have the foolish notion that the only way they can live for God is by becoming ministers, missionaries, or Bible teachers. Think of how many would be shut out from any opportunity of magnifying the Most High if this were the case! Beloved, it is not your calling; it is earnestness. It is not your position; it is grace that will enable us to glorify God. God is most surely glorified in that cobbler's stall, where the godly worker, as he plies the awl, sings of the Savior's love. He is glorified far more there than in many churches where official religiousness performs its scanty duties. The name of Jesus is glorified by the poor, unlearned peddler, as he drives his horse and blesses his God or speaks to his fellow laborer by the roadside, as much as by the popular clergyman who, throughout the country, like Boanerges, is thundering out the Gospel. God is glorified by our serving Him in our proper vocations. Take care, dear reader, that you do not forsake the path of duty by leaving your occupation, and take care that you do not dishonor your profession while in it. Think little of yourselves, but do not think too little of your calling. Every lawful trade may be sanctified by the Gospel to the noblest ends. Turn to the Bible, and you will find the most menial forms of labor connected either with the most daring deeds of faith or with persons whose lives have been illustrious for holiness. Therefore, do not be discontented with your calling. Whatever God has made your position or your work, abide in that, unless you are quite sure that He calls you to something else. Let your first care be to glorify God to the utmost of your power where you are. Fill your present sphere to His praise, and if He needs you in another place, He will show it to you. This evening, lay aside distressing ambition, and embrace peaceful contentment.

```
A P A W K Z P G N U Q V A S X D R G Q O
G H M N N M I N I S T E R S G J K L S L
U N B P N V O C A T I O N S M Q E O W T
N J I L U K J C V N D N O Y I G F R F G
L G T B W D U Z Y G Q N Q R S M R I L P
E I I Z J E T X X S W K K S C L F R O
A F O O P P O R T U N I T Y I V Q Y J C
R H N Y G H Z E Z U M P F N O N E H H C
N A B P W V K U M X N U J W N O D S O U
E O T Y P W K Y R P C R M T A T N P R P
D X R D I S T R E S S I N G R I A E S A
O F Z D D H M O S T L J F S I O V D E T
F P T V H L R O A D S I D E E N Q D O I
Q L T F R Y Y F R O Q Z Q G S Y B L Q O
M O L Q G L S C Z L C F J F V O Z E E N
T E A C H E R S I F X L F O N C I R K S
H I G H R U M A G N I F Y I N G N B Z H
W T W I M P W P G V B N X T V W E D Y K
R E L I G I O U S N E S S C A N T Y E A
P S E F N C C Q U C O B B L E R B B I K
```

NOTION	MINISTERS	MISSIONARIES	TEACHERS
OPPORTUNITY	MAGNIFYING	MOST	HIGH
GLORIFY	COBBLER	RELIGIOUSNESS	SCANTY
UNLEARNED	PEDDLER	HORSE	ROADSIDE
VOCATIONS	OCCUPATION	DISTRESSING	AMBITION

Morning

In summer and in winter shall it be.
—Zechariah 14:8

The streams of living water that flow from Jerusalem are not dried up by the parching heat of sultry midsummer any more than they were frozen by the cold winds of blustering winter. Rejoice, O my soul, that you are spared to testify of the faithfulness of the Lord. The seasons change and you change, but your Lord abides evermore the same, and the streams of His love are as deep, as broad, and as full as ever. The pressures of business cares and scorching trials make me need the cooling influences of the river of His grace. I may go at once and drink to the full from the inexhaustible fountain, for in summer and in winter it pours forth its flood. The upper springs are never scanty, and, blessed be the name of the Lord, the lower springs cannot fail either. Elijah found Cherith dried up, but Jehovah was still the same God of providence. Job said his brethren were like deceitful brooks, but he found his God an overflowing river of consolation. The Nile is the great confidence of Egypt, but its floods are variable; our Lord is evermore the same. By turning the course of the Euphrates, Cyrus took the city of Babylon, but no power, human or infernal, can divert the current of divine grace. The tracks of ancient rivers have been found all dry and desolate, but the streams that take their rise on the mountains of divine sovereignty and infinite love will ever be full to the brim. Generations melt away, but the course of grace is unaltered. The river of God may sing with greater truth than the brook in the poem,

Men may come, and men may go,
　But I go on forever.

How happy are you, my soul, to be led beside such still waters! Never wander to other streams, lest you hear the Lord's rebuke, "Why go to Egypt to drink from the muddy river?" (See Jeremiah 2:18.)

```
T W T Z C W Z V A D P O C C J I A O F X
A I J S O J N O A X K E F H O L H L M U
J N B C N N A Q S E Y V O G R L B N M V
Q T Z O S O L F F Q O E U X Q X D A I R
G E F R O U U U R Z L R N U K B P R D H
S R P C L A F B P L N M T X I E N Q S A
G K M H A Z R S B H X O A F P S G X U A
F B N I T B L U S T E R I N G N Z P M B
K S T N I L W O E I T E N P E H X R M I
L I F G O A P Q L G R B T K Y H L E E D
N D A D N E B C D A I R I Z Z Z B S R E
S W X L F K D D R J A O U H D S E S E S
K Q B W D R D M J Q L A E E Q G G U E V
C H A N G E O G S T S D B A R C U R C Y
I X S U R R Z Z Q V R Q Y T T I F E O M
W C I V J Q V V E Y N B F S P Y V S K P
B K V C Z Y C I J N Y K Q P H J B E B D
V K M I N E X H A U S T I B L E I Q R S
D Q D R I E D I H S U L T R Y I X Y J M
J O X Y C C A R E S Z G C I N B M J N V
```

DRIED   HEAT   SULTRY   MIDSUMMER

FROZEN   COLD   BLUSTERING   WINTER

CHANGE   ABIDES   EVERMORE   BROAD

PRESSURES   CARES   SCORCHING   TRIALS

INEXHAUSTIBLE   FOUNTAIN   RIVER   CONSOLATION

Evening

They heard the voice of the Lord God
walking in the garden in the cool of the day.
—Genesis 3:8

My soul, now that the *"cool of the day"* has come, go to a quiet place and listen to the voice of your God. He is always ready to speak with you when you are prepared to hear. If you find that communion with God is slow in coming, the problem is not on His part but altogether on your own. For He stands at the door and knocks, and if His people will only open to Him, He will rejoice to enter. Yet in what state is my heart, which is my Lord's garden? May I venture to hope that it is well trimmed and watered and is bringing forth fruit fit for Him? If not, He will have much about which to reprove me. Yet I still ask Him to come to me, for nothing can so certainly bring my heart into a right condition as the presence of the Sun of Righteousness, who brings *"healing in his wings"* (Mal. 4:2). Come, therefore, O Lord my God; my soul invites You earnestly and waits for You eagerly. Come to me, O Jesus, my Well Beloved, and plant fresh flowers in my garden, such as I see blooming in perfection in Your matchless character. Come, O my Father. You are the Husbandman; deal with me in Your tenderness and prudence. Come, O Holy Spirit, and let Your dew fall on my whole nature, as the herbs are now moistened with the evening dews. Oh, that God would speak to me! *"Speak, Lord; for thy servant heareth"* (1 Sam. 3:9). Oh, that He would walk with me! I am ready to give up my whole heart and mind to Him, and every other thought is hushed. I only ask what He delights to give. I am sure that He will, in His grace, have fellowship with me, for He has given me His Holy Spirit to be with me forever. Sweet is the cool twilight, when every star seems like the eye of heaven and the cool wind is as the breath of divine love. My Father, my Elder Brother, my sweet Comforter, speak now in lovingkindness, for You have *"opened mine ear, and I [am] not rebellious"* (Isa. 50:5).

```
O G G W Y R G S M V L S X V Z V F O J D
I Y L I S T E N V M H Q H Z H B O P S P
D M Q T M T F D K O P Q U I E T V F T T
H O K C O O L I W S O B L S S F I N A T
R H O R E A D Y K R D F E L D E R X N V
D M H R S U K I Y N S F X D U U R U D K
J P C R I G X T Y F O X L W X I M N S D
T W I L I G H T X E L C J O F R G A A F
B C P Q L E H K L A Y G K I I M N A A H
P R U D E N C E I A L T O G E T H E R U
G M E E R F J B Z U I N L B F P E Q D S
E K L O O B J C S L I O Q V M U Z P K H
I H F B N B N B O O Q O U S X M X C R E
B B U N P O X Y Q Y M A T C H L E S S D
P R E P A R E D M C T Q Q A O Z T T K D
P W B T O K T C G B R O T H E R U A A M
V J V P V O O Y Q L G X A J K U I T I O
L L S O T O L R X R E P R O V E X E H X
W T N P R O B L E M M T F H E A R O Q F
Z J D F G W O P E N J Z B Z M D U V W W
```

COOL   QUIET   LISTEN   READY
PREPARED   HEAR   PROBLEM   ALTOGETHER
STANDS   DOOR   KNOCK   OPEN
STATE   REPROVE   MATCHLESS   PRUDENCE
HUSHED   TWILIGHT   ELDER   BROTHER

Morning

Brethren, pray for us.
—1 Thessalonians 5:25

We reserved this one morning in the year to refresh the reader's memory on the subject of prayer for ministers, and we most earnestly implore every Christian household to grant the fervent request of the text first uttered by an apostle and now repeated by us. Brethren, our work is solemnly momentous, involving well-being or woe to thousands. We deal with souls for God on eternal business, and our word is either the aroma of life to life, or of death to death. A very heavy responsibility rests on us, and it will be no small mercy if at the last we are found clear of the blood of all men. As officers in Christ's army, we are the special target of the hatred of men and devils; they watch for our halting and labor to take us by the heels. Our sacred calling involves us in temptations from which you are exempt. Above all it too often draws us away from our personal enjoyment of truth into a ministerial and official consideration of it. We meet with many knotty cases, and our wits are confounded. We observe very sad backslidings, and our hearts are wounded; we see millions perishing, and our spirits sink. We wish to benefit you by our preaching. We desire to be a blessing to your children. We long to be useful both to saints and sinners; therefore, dear friends, intercede for us with our God. Miserable men are we if we miss the aid of your prayers, but happy are we if we live in your supplications. You do not look to us but to our Master for spiritual blessings, and yet how many times has He given those blessings through His ministers. Ask, then, again and again, that we may be the earthen vessels into which the Lord may put the treasure of the Gospel. We, the whole company of missionaries, ministers, city missionaries, and students, do in the name of Jesus beseech you, *"Brethren, pray for us."*

```
H E A V Y J L Z Q C O N F O U N D E D H
R V T J B Y C P S A Z Q J M N C B M U M
M A T J H D K L Q D A T M P J O R O B I
W O E L X F J M E Z N I I L U G E M Q S
B J R F E L F G P A J S Q X A M T E O E
A P K T E I W Y Y A R Y S E U F H N J R
N R S K Q R E S U O K N O T T Y E T Z A
R A O I N T E R C E D E K D C U R O D B
Q L K M J H I R H A T R E D E L E U E L
H I Y M A N F L I A N Z S C S K N S V E
P I E G W O P G E Y T Z Z Z Q N J Y I P
E X E M P T Q A F Q B U I P V A E P L S
V J W F S M I L L I O N S S C V H L S D
P A L M I N I S T E R I A L S K N B T S
B A C K S L I D I N G S I L D W T L Q L
Z L M U K A Q C P E Q T U T A R G E T N
G G F M J R C B K M I K M K Z I F E B I
U Y I Y N M D H T S J I M P L O R E N M
A L Y R X Y A K L T E J E B R A U S P X
W E E P H S O L E M N L L Y U C X Y G T
```

IMPLORE	BRETHREN	SOLEMNLY	MOMENTOUS
WOE	AROMA	HEAVY	CLEAR
ARMY	TARGET	HATRED	DEVILS
EXEMPT	MINISTERIAL	KNOTTY	CONFOUNDED
BACKSLIDINGS	MILLIONS	INTERCEDE	MISERABLE

Evening

When I passed by thee,…I said unto thee…, Live.
—Ezekiel 16:6

Saved one, consider gratefully this command of mercy in our text. Note first that this command of God is majestic. We perceive a sinner with nothing in him but sin, and expecting nothing but wrath. However, the eternal Lord passes by in His glory. He looks, He pauses, and He pronounces the solitary but royal word, *"Live."* There speaks a God. Who but He could thus venture to deal with life and dispense it with a single syllable? Second, this command is manifold. When He says, *"Live,"* His command includes many things. It is judicial life. The sinner is ready to be condemned, but the mighty One says, *"Live,"* and so he rises pardoned and absolved. It is spiritual life. Before we knew Jesus, our eyes could not see Him, and our ears could not hear His voice. Yet Jehovah said, *"Live,"* and we were *"quickened, who were dead in trespasses and sins"* (Eph. 2:1). Moreover, it is glory life, which is the perfection of spiritual life. *"I said unto thee…, Live."* This last word rolls on through all the years of time until death comes, and in the midst of the shadows of death, the Lord's voice is still heard: *"Live."* On the morning of the resurrection to life, this same word will be echoed by the archangel: *"Live."* As holy spirits rise to heaven to be blessed forever in the glory of their God, it will be in the power of this very word, *"Live."* Third, it is an irresistible command. Saul of Tarsus was on the road to Damascus to arrest the children of the living God. He heard a voice from heaven and saw a light brighter than the sun, and he cried out, *"Lord, what wilt thou have me to do?"* (Acts 9:6). Fourth, it is a command of free grace. When sinners are saved, God saves them solely to glorify His free, unpurchased, unsought grace. Christians, recognize your position: you are debtors to grace. Since God has commanded you to live, show your gratitude by living earnest, Christlike lives.

```
V D I S P E N S E P M J X Z M B B K W X
N E Z G A C S B H E E U K Y I P W R Z G
B O N C P T I O Q X C R M T D B O S G J
I Y N T T G C C L X E J C C G B T A X M
X P H I U K R Y U I X U I E N X L R U F
X X F R I R D A S V T D B Q I Z V C Y H
P Z L N P E E R T K A A R M Q V S H A Q
O S H A D O W S I E N B R U V H E A B Y
U C S Y L L A B L E F B M Y T Z N N S T
N V W O J I X L Y I I U U H Q Q P G O R
O P A R D O N E D N M J L M X W U E L E
C O N D E M N E D F U S R L Y V Z L V S
M T F Y F Y P S L S F W N U Y N N F E P
I W B K O J E H O V A H J I V F X W D A
G T Y F Q N H Q L G O P G B N Y E R B S
H M S D I S R I C O S A V E D L N A N S
T K D D V A P M A J E S T I C L K T Y E
Y D K U S M A N I F O L D E R T W H D S
U Z C O R P A L N F J U D I C I A L D C
M Y N Y W Q U I C K E N E D G X G W N J
```

SAVED	GRATEFULLY	MAJESTIC	PERCEIVE
WRATH	SOLITARY	VENTURE	DISPENSE
SYLLABLE	MANIFOLD	JUDICIAL	CONDEMNED
MIGHTY	PARDONED	ABSOLVED	JEHOVAH
QUICKENED	TRESPASSES	SHADOWS	ARCHANGEL

Morning

The LORD our God hath showed us his glory.
—Deuteronomy 5:24

God's great design in all His works is the manifestation of His own glory. Any aim less than this would be unworthy of Him. But how will the glory of God be manifested to such fallen creatures as we are? Man's eye is not single; he always has a side-glance toward his own honor. He has too high an estimate of his own powers, and so he is not qualified to behold the glory of the Lord. It is clear, then, that self must stand out of the way, so that there may be room for God to be exalted. This is the reason that He often brings His people into problems and difficulties, so that, being made conscious of their own folly and weakness, they may be fitted to behold the majesty of God when He comes forth to work their deliverance. He whose life is one even, smooth path will see only a little of the glory of the Lord, for he has few occasions of self-emptying; hence, he has only a little fitness for being filled with the revelation of God. Those who navigate little streams and shallow creeks know little of the God of tempests, but those who "*do business in great waters*" (Ps. 107:23) see "*his wonders in the deep*" (v. 24). Among the huge Atlantic waves of bereavement, poverty, temptation, and reproach, we learn the power of Jehovah, because we feel the inadequacy of man. Thank God, then, if you have been led by a rough road. It is this that has given you your experience of God's greatness and lovingkindness. Your troubles have enriched you with a wealth of knowledge to be gained by no other means. Your trials have been the cleft of the rock in which Jehovah has set you, as He did His servant Moses, so that you might behold His glory as it passes by. Praise God that you have not been left to the darkness and ignorance that continued prosperity might have involved, but that in the great fight of affliction, you have been equipped for the outshinings of His glory in His wonderful dealings with you.

```
N L U N C T V Q S N I S E S W R E W X Q
I V N W Y Y T O C S X L S S N T S T A T
G L A N C E N Y D C R N H W G Q T Y Y B
H F B S M O O T H W Y N I L Y W I G F O
C O N S C I O U S A C A A D M L M W I O
Q F Y P R E A S O N F G D V U J A E T M
S H A L L O W K A D Q X L N I A T Q T N
P T D I F F I C U L T I E S R G E L E R
U C N S O C N K P C M G O T D K A Z D R
O X S O B B R Y H F K R Y E X A L T D J
U C M F Y D U C I Q D Z J Y D W G W E W
O M A N I F E S T A T I O N N T D O S E
E S O R A D M Q Y A T L S S H S H R O A
H X Q U A L I F I E D R A U U B O K B K
S D E L I V E R A N C E X K G K U S W N
U F J C R E E K S D R P P B K H W Z Z E
K X N X L Z D V A K W C Q L G R E A T S
M P W T Z X K R P R Q C B G D X P I R S
X I M L O R E V E L A T I O N Q F M Q Y
E E M U E F O L B T O W A R D W N V E N
```

GREAT	WORKS	MANIFESTATION	AIM
GLANCE	TOWARD	ESTIMATE	QUALIFIED
EXALTED	REASON	DIFFICULTIES	CONSCIOUS
WEAKNESS	FITTED	DELIVERANCE	SMOOTH
REVELATION	NAVIGATE	SHALLOW	CREEKS

Evening

A bruised reed shall he not break,
and smoking flax shall he not quench.
—Matthew 12:20

What is weaker than a bruised reed or smoking flax? If a wild duck merely lands on a reed that grows in a swamp or marsh, the reed will snap. If someone's foot brushes against it, it will become bruised or broken. Every wind that flits across the river moves it back and forth. One can conceive of nothing more frail or brittle, or whose existence is more in jeopardy, than a bruised reed. Now consider smoking flax—what is it? It is true that it has a spark within it. However, it is almost smothered; an infant's breath might blow it out. Nothing has a more precarious existence than its flame. Weak things are being described in our text, yet Jesus says of them, "The smoking flax I will not quench; the bruised reed I will not break." Some of God's children have been made strong to do mighty works for Him. God has His Samsons here and there who can pull up Gaza's gates and carry them to the top of the hill. He has a few mighty believers who are lionlike, but the majority of His people are a timid, trembling race. They are like starlings, frightened at every passerby; they are a fearful little flock. If temptation comes, they are taken like birds in a snare; if trial threatens, they are ready to faint. Their frail little boat is tossed up and down by every wave; they drift along like a seabird on the crest of the billows. They are weak things, without strength, without wisdom, and without foresight. Yet, weak as they are, and *because* they are so weak, this promise is made especially to them. Herein is grace and graciousness! Herein is love and lovingkindness! How it reveals to us the compassion of Jesus—so gentle, tender, and considerate. We never need to shrink back from His touch. We never need to fear a harsh word from Him. Although He may well chide us for our weakness, He does not rebuke us. Bruised reeds will receive no blows from Him, and smoking flax will receive no quenching frowns.

```
Z  J  E  O  P  A  R  D  Y  M  U  I  G  O  H  O  F  O  B  D
E  B  R  O  K  E  N  M  B  T  Q  R  J  W  H  J  O  B  R  R
E  X  I  S  T  E  N  C  E  X  U  X  S  G  S  S  L  R  I  Z
X  F  Y  C  H  X  E  Y  D  M  E  Y  T  L  M  Y  L  P  T  F
N  R  O  B  G  M  T  P  U  U  N  F  A  D  O  M  E  F  T  G
J  A  Y  J  V  P  B  G  W  B  C  D  R  Q  K  I  T  Q  L  D
X  I  L  I  O  N  L  I  K  E  H  O  L  X  I  D  T  L  E  C
F  L  T  U  M  D  W  L  N  P  I  Y  I  Z  N  U  W  R  F  P
Z  B  G  Q  I  N  Y  Y  S  V  N  V  N  H  G  L  D  R  X  R
S  M  O  T  H  E  R  E  D  B  G  G  G  T  V  V  R  Y  T  E
S  D  O  I  N  Q  Y  E  V  O  B  R  S  A  R  D  A  T  S  C
G  S  N  U  T  Y  X  V  U  O  P  O  S  H  R  B  E  O  C  A
V  T  F  B  R  U  I  S  E  D  A  Y  Y  F  R  E  E  D  V  R
J  I  U  H  P  C  F  C  T  F  E  O  F  R  O  W  N  S  Q  I
T  S  F  M  O  Q  K  L  M  L  L  S  W  A  M  P  O  U  V  O
N  J  L  G  G  Q  C  S  A  H  Z  I  S  I  A  A  J  L  A  U
L  P  V  L  I  Q  O  W  X  X  Z  J  T  C  L  J  Q  T  W  S
O  Z  M  V  I  N  X  E  I  O  X  Y  Y  S  R  D  P  H  M  U
K  D  E  Z  X  H  C  L  V  C  J  X  O  M  I  I  J  U  W  A
T  K  N  D  S  O  A  C  D  U  C  K  Q  M  A  R  S  H  W  U
```

BRUISED	REED	SMOKING	FLAX
WILD	DUCK	SWAMP	MARSH
BROKEN	FLITS	FRAIL	BRITTLE
EXISTENCE	JEOPARDY	SMOTHERED	PRECARIOUS
LIONLIKE	STARLINGS	QUENCHING	FROWNS

Morning

I am married unto you.
—Jeremiah 3:14

Christ Jesus is joined with His people in the union of marriage. In love He espoused His church as a chaste virgin, long before she fell under the yoke of bondage. Full of burning affection, Christ toiled, like Jacob for Rachel, until the whole of her purchase-money had been paid. And now, having sought her by His Spirit, and brought her to know and love Him, Christ awaits the glorious hour when their mutual bliss will be consummated at the Marriage Supper of the Lamb. Not yet has the glorious Bridegroom presented His betrothed, perfected and complete, before the Majesty of heaven; not yet has she actually entered into the enjoyment of her privileges as His wife and queen. She is as yet a wanderer in a world of woe, a dweller *"in the tents of Kedar"* (Ps. 120:5); but she is even now the bride, the spouse of Jesus, dear to His heart, precious in His sight, written on His hands, and united with His person. On earth He exercises toward her all the affectionate offices of Husband. He makes rich provision for her needs, pays all her debts, and allows her to assume His name and to share in all His wealth. Nor will He ever act otherwise to her. The word *divorce* He will never mention, for He *"hateth putting away"* (Mal. 2:16). Death must sever the conjugal tie between the most loving mortals, but it cannot divide the links of this immortal marriage. In heaven they do not marry, but are as the angels of God; yet there is this one marvelous exception to the rule, for in heaven Christ and His church will celebrate their joyous nuptials. Because this affinity is more lasting, it is more intimate than earthly wedlock. Although the love of a husband may be so pure and fervent, it is but a faint picture of the flame that burns in the heart of Jesus. Surpassing all human union is that mystical cleaving unto the church, for which Christ left His Father and became one flesh with her.

```
O J A Y R Q F O M M A R R I A G E R N X
L J N B O M X K S J Z Y E K E V U C T G
X O I I B K C C P L N C D H W C U I Z I
I I A Z U D E Q K N N J W U K O R O P Q
L N E J R F J G O H Y P J S N N A A E F
Z P R G N K E D A R U K Q B X S C U R N
N I D W I D J R J V K P V A M U H C F K
W I F E N Y B O N D A G E N V M E S E Q
N L D N G Y H H H N D B O D C M L M C Y
Z U S B L L R T O H M E X A O A C M T K
V T T D T M Y B B Z M T L L M T Q F E X
J U O P B M W F Y G D R N P P E P N D U
O G N U M M D R X O Z O J U L D X W B P
I U K I P U F Y A S V T Q R E P S Z R Y
N E G B O T X K T W B H G C T C F J A Y
E D B J F N U F G B G E A H E I C W V J
D W M U T U A L L E R D Z A B Z J E Q F
G D W E L L E R J P U H X S W V H T Q U
P A E Z X S S S Y D W P M E M O N E Y P
E S P O U S E D B R I D E G R O O M L G
```

JOINED	UNION	MARRIAGE	ESPOUSED
YOKE	BONDAGE	BURNING	RACHEL
PURCHASE	MONEY	MUTUAL	CONSUMMATED
BRIDEGROOM	BETROTHED	PERFECTED	COMPLETE
WIFE	DWELLER	KEDAR	HUSBAND

Evening

Behold the man!
—John 19:5

If there is one place where our Lord Jesus most fully became the joy and comfort of His people, it is where He plunged deepest into the depths of woe. Come, gracious souls, and *"behold the man"* in the Garden of Gethsemane. See His heart brimming so full of love that He cannot hold it in—and so full of sorrow that it must find release. See the bloody sweat as it drips from every pore of His body and falls to the ground. *"Behold the man"* as they drive the nails into His hands and feet. Look up, repenting sinners, and see the sorrowful image of your suffering Lord on the cross. Notice how the ruby drops of blood stand on the crown of thorns and adorn, as if priceless gems, the diadem of the King of Misery. *"Behold the man"* when all His bones are out of joint, and He is poured out like water and brought into the dust of death. God forsook Him and hell surrounded Him. Look and see: did anyone else ever sorrow as He sorrowed? All you who pass by, draw near and look upon this spectacle of grief—unique, unparalleled, a wonder to men and angels. Behold the Emperor of Woe, who has no equal or rival in His agonies! Gaze on Him, you mourners, for if there is no consolation in a crucified Christ, there is no joy on earth or in heaven. If there is no hope in the ransom-price of His blood, there is no joy in the harps of heaven, and the right hand of God will never know any pleasures. If we would sit more often at the foot of the cross, we would be less troubled with our doubts and sorrows. If we see His sorrows, we will be ashamed to mention our sorrows. If we but gaze into His wounds, our wounds will be healed. If we want to live right, it must be by the contemplation of His death. If we want to rise to dignity, it must be by considering His humiliation and sorrow.

```
X V F V B H L W P X I R E L E A S E E A
W Q S W E A T I W C I Y V A K D W Z J P
X O R X D A A J O J U O G A W E F O U T
F E X Y C M D Z O D R A F V S E A G N U
P G R U B X L Q J S L S Y C Z P M B A L
G C O M F O R T U P M U M W C E O R R B
R N A Y S J I P J L A I E K O S Z I A L
K I G C C C B Z U R T C X N T R M L O
V J R G A G H J D N N D Y R T B L M L O
S R J G H N E G G O Y V Z E I W I E D
X I O E U E N N F E B F G Q M P H N L Y
J A N D V G U O X D Q F I Y P O Z G E N
I K N N E P E Z T C P Y R L L R A I D X
T H I A E P H A A P H X G L A E S B E F
W Z U F W R T D R I P S N I T F O H U U
C V P Q V Z S H T W E C N N I O O K J L
P O W O U N D S S E G G C M O D M S N L
C J Y Z G L I B M H M T A T N K U B I Y
A D I A D E M W Z R E P E N T I N G R L
D A S H A M E D Y S V I G A Z E L R V V
```

FULLY	COMFORT	PLUNGED	DEEPEST
DEPTHS	BRIMMING	CANNOT	RELEASE
BLOODY	SWEAT	DRIPS	PORE
REPENTING	SINNERS	DIADEM	UNPARALLELED
ASHAMED	GAZE	WOUNDS	CONTEMPLATION

Morning

Who worketh all things after the counsel of his own will.
—Ephesians 1:11

Our belief in God's wisdom supposes and necessitates that He has a settled purpose and plan in the work of salvation. What would Creation have been without His design? Is there a fish in the sea or a fowl in the air that was left to chance for its formation? No, in every bone, joint, muscle, sinew, gland, and blood vessel, you observe the presence of a God working everything according to the design of infinite wisdom. And will God be present in creation, ruling over all, and not in grace? Will the new creation have the fickle genius of free will to preside over it when divine counsel rules the old creation? Look at Providence! Who does not know that not even a sparrow falls to the ground without your Father's knowledge? Even the hairs of your head are all numbered. God weighs the mountains of our grief on scales, and the hills of our tribulation on balances. And will there be a God in providence and not in grace? Will the shell be ordained by wisdom and the kernel be left to blind chance? No, He knows the end from the beginning. He sees in its appointed place, not merely the Cornerstone, which He has laid in fair colors in the blood of His dear Son, but He beholds in their ordained position each of the chosen stones taken out of the quarry of nature and polished by His grace. He sees the whole from corner to cornice, from base to roof, from foundation to pinnacle. He has in His mind a clear knowledge of every stone that will be laid in its prepared space, how vast the edifice will be, and when the top-stone will be brought forth with shoutings of "Grace! Grace! unto it." At the last it will be clearly seen that in every chosen vessel of mercy, Jehovah did as He willed with His own; and that in every part of the work of grace, He accomplished His purposes and glorified His own name.

```
N P Y W S L A I R P F D A B F F B C O C
R R X W B P F E O I T G F J O Z A S P O
E P D V E Z A M O N U B O C U P B K P R
G D I P H Z I C F N H N R Z N M P K S N
O P I A W W Z S E A U Y M J D U S N U I
R N Y F F A P D E C O D A P A S Q F P C
C D C A I R H S H L T Z T U T C R K P E
J O I N T C T B H E N L I R I L E N O Z
Y E E Z G E E S E O U A P O E X V S L
Y S D Q X L F K Y L U E N O N A K D E F
K S W N N T V L B O I T C S R Z H J S I
N Q K N H G H G P S K E I E G K K Y F U
K H Q S B Q N K L M Q S F N Y T U X S Q
S S E T T L E D G A O E C A G E S A O P
Q T A U T I D N U D N J M Y Q S I R S I
H I O M G M P N Y O C D S K P D N O Z A
M F A N L C O R N E R Z C T K Z E U A G
S K F U E N L Z Q D X I L B R W W D G B
R Z N E C E S S I T A T E S V Q Y I O E
C K Q A X X R H A M D R V L D B A S E K
```

BELIEF SUPPOSES NECESSITATES SETTLED

PURPOSE FORMATION JOINT MUSCLE

SINEW GLAND CORNER CORNICE

BASE ROOF FOUNDATION PINNACLE

STONE SPACE EDIFICE SHOUTINGS

Evening

So she gleaned in the field until even.
—Ruth 2:17

Let me learn from Ruth, the gleaner. As she went out to gather ears of corn, so I must go out into the fields of prayer, meditation, doctrine, and the hearing of the Word, in order to gather spiritual food. The gleaner gathers her portion ear by ear; her gains are little by little. I must be content to search for single truths, if there is no greater abundance of them. Every ear helps to make a bundle, and every gospel lesson assists in making us *"wise unto salvation"* (2 Tim. 3:15). The gleaner keeps her eyes open. If she were to stumble along the fields while daydreaming, she would have no load to carry home in the evening. I must be watchful while engaging in religious disciplines, so that they will not become unprofitable to me. I fear I have lost much already. Oh, that I may rightly estimate my opportunities and glean with greater diligence! The gleaner stoops for all she finds, and so must I. Haughty spirits criticize and object, but humble minds glean and receive benefit. A humble heart is a great help toward profitably hearing the Gospel. The soul-saving *"engrafted word"* (James 1:21) is not received except with meekness. A stiff back makes for bad gleaning. Pride is a vile robber, not to be endured for a moment. What the gleaner gathers, she holds. If she were to drop one ear to find another, the result of her day's work would be meager. She is as careful to retain as to obtain, so that in the end her gains are great. How often do I forget all that I hear; a second truth pushes the first out of my head, and so my reading and hearing end in much ado about nothing! Do I have the proper conviction of the importance of storing up the truth? A hungry stomach makes the gleaner wise. If there is no corn in her hand, there will be no bread on her table. She labors under a sense of necessity; therefore, she walks nimbly, and her grasp is firm. I have an even greater need. Lord, help me to be convinced of this need, so that it may urge me onward to glean in fields that yield so plenteous a reward to diligence.

```
P S E V U B V Q H G A T H E R F D J T F
H T L P S G U T O A N M X K A Z O X J H
Y U X L N S L I C Z Z S Z B F J C I M M
E M N H O H T E F F I E L D S P T S U E
M B J G S V W O A U D L U E U C R C O E
P L S M R A V M M N B W G A M T I L Y K
H E D S L Y J L T A E A J R C U N C K N
Q D A M F A W P G G C R A S R N E Y A E
K E R G T K L R M L W H T M E P Y N H S
Y R Q O C O N V I N C E D N O R R N F S
N H A U G H T Y Q K K V M J G O Q S D E
W I T U Z A W S L X J H N P Q F R K I Z
W P M J Z U L S T O R I N G V I R W L T
M C B B E S Y T H H M L M P K T D O I N
R D U L L K V W J T R C T X E A W N G N
O S D I M Y Q O R U U U Q B S B O W E X
L R E W A R D Y U T T I G E F L G A N L
T G Y B K P Q S A X H J P U M E U R C A
K P L D W D Y M E D I T A T I O N D E E
Z K U P V O F D A Y D R E A M I N G M M
```

RUTH	GLEANER	GATHER	EARS
MEDITATION	DOCTRINE	STUMBLE	DAYDREAMING
UNPROFITABLE	HAUGHTY	MEEKNESS	STORING
HUNGRY	STOMACH	NIMBLY	CONVINCED
ONWARD	FIELDS	REWARD	DILIGENCE

Morning

We know that all things work together for good
to them that love God.
—Romans 8:28

On some points a believer is absolutely sure. He knows, for instance, that God sits with the passengers of the vessel when it rocks the most. He believes that an invisible hand is always on the world's tiller, and that wherever providence may lead the vessel, Jehovah steers it. That reassuring knowledge prepares him for everything. He looks over the raging waters and sees the spirit of Jesus treading the billows. He hears a voice saying, *"It is I; be not afraid"* (Matt. 14:27). He knows, too, that God is always wise; knowing this, he is confident that there can be no accidents, no mistakes. Nothing can occur that should not happen. He can say, "If I would lose all that I have, it is better that I should lose it than keep it, if God so wills. The worst calamity is the wisest and the kindest thing that could happen to me if God ordains it." *"We know that all things work together for good to them that love God."* The Christian does not merely hold this as a theory, but he knows it as a matter of fact. Everything has worked for good so far. The poisonous drugs mixed in proper proportions have worked the cure; the sharp cuts of the scalpel have cleansed out the ulcerous flesh and facilitated the healing. Every event thus far has worked out the most divinely blessed results. And so, believing that God rules all, that He governs wisely, that He brings good out of evil, the believer's heart is assured, and he is enabled calmly to meet each trial as it comes. The believer can in the spirit of true resignation pray, "Send me what You will, my God, as long as it comes from You. A bad portion has never come from Your table to any of Your children." Do not say, my soul,

From whence can God relieve my care?

Remember that Omnipotence has servants everywhere.

His method is sublime; His heart profoundly kind.

God never is before His time and never is behind.

```
A P R O F O U N D L Y R S T W K I H S E
R A G I N G Q S T R G U R T G B W A C K
L R J J B J C U B Y F L H U E L Y S A F
H Q O G T E X B S K A C M L N E T H L A
A C T C H G F L D Q L E E J O K R R P C
W B H D K N S I T R G R P Q R O E S E I
W E E E I S S M G C Z O A Y M J A R L L
C B O N E U P E K E S U N R K J D W H I
K U R W H E N C E L B S U X A I I C O T
D B Y B W N R E A S S U R I N G N A T A
P D M I S T A K E S A Q J A W S G L O T
N D E B X J Q C L E P C W D V H C A G E
P A S S E N G E R S Q C C Q I P D M J D
F R N U L Z H M P A A V C I I D U I T C
P U M O D Z H L U W D V U X D H G T V T
W P O I S O N O U S M G F E N E X Y K V
G L Z B G F O W F N S E Z P J L N A I Z
W J W R L J C O N F I D E N T K X T U S
X E F W U Z P R O V I D E N C E O V H S
J S B S I N V I S I B L E S B A C E K M
```

PASSENGERS	ROCKS	INVISIBLE	PROVIDENCE
STEERS	REASSURING	RAGING	TREADING
CONFIDENT	ACCIDENT	MISTAKES	CALAMITY
THEORY	POISONOUS	SCALPEL	ULCEROUS
FACILITATED	WHENCE	SUBLIME	PROFOUNDLY

Evening

Shall your brethren go to war, and shall ye sit here?
—Numbers 32:6

Family relationships have their obligations. The Reubenites and Gadites would have been unbrotherly if they had claimed the land that had been conquered, but had left the rest of the people to fight for their own land (Joshua 1:12–16). We in the church have received much by means of the efforts and sufferings of the saints in years past. If we do not make some repayment to the church of Christ by giving her our best energies, we are unworthy to be enrolled in her ranks. Others are combating the errors of the age manfully or excavating perishing ones from amid the ruins of the Fall. If we fold our hands in idleness, we must be warned, lest the curse of Meroz falls upon us. (See Judges 5:23.) The Master of the vineyard says, *"Why stand ye here all the day idle?"* (Matt. 20:6). What is the idler's excuse? Personal service for Jesus becomes all the more the duty of everyone because it is cheerfully and abundantly offered by some. The efforts of devoted missionaries and fervent ministers shame us if we sit in laziness. Shrinking from trial is the temptation of those who are *"at ease in Zion"* (Amos 6:1). They would be happy to escape the cross, yet wear the crown. To them, the question of this evening's meditation is very applicable. If the most precious of God's servants are tried in the fire, can we expect to escape the crucible? If a diamond must be distressed while it is being cleaved, cut, and polished, are we to be made perfect without suffering? Do we expect the wind to cease from blowing simply because our ship is at sea? Why should we be treated better than our Lord? If the Firstborn felt the rod, why shouldn't His younger brothers and sisters? It is cowardly pride that would choose a soft pillow and bed for a soldier of the Cross. Far wiser is the person who first submits to the divine will and then grows to be pleased with it through the operations of grace. He will learn to gather lilies at the foot of the cross and, like Samson, to find honey in the lion. (See Judges 14:1–9.)

```
C O P E R A T I O N S Z B L G R V N U U
C P E R I S H I N G B S X M K A G R W M
J V Y E H L J M U V P O R O E X B E M A
T V Y X Q U N B R O T H E R L Y C P A B
X C K C R W V O Q Q K E Y F P G R A N C
P T A A J E E N R O L L E D M X U Y F O
O E W V P J L C G T A T U N D A C M U M
A O T A P J E A A S A M S O N X I E L B
H L T T Q R Z Q T J C L P G I I B N L A
L A Z I N E S S M I G S O M Z P L T Y T
H J L N A K S U V V O D L Q X X E I L I
R L U G I H D A Z M R N I J T I H D X N
N O Q R N T B V U S I R S N F P Q L X G
S H R E U B E N I T E S H H J Q A E P O
Z L S H C U S P U H F P E X I S V N M L
X B S U Z T B M E R O Z D D Y P O E J E
Q B D X G A D I T E S M L Y B E S S W T
I Q Y X V D I A M O N D W E W M T S I R
B G V T Y O B L I G A T I O N S W K J X
V S P T I W P R E N E R G I E S T I W G
```

RELATIONSHIPS   OBLIGATIONS   REUBENITES   GADITES
UNBROTHERLY   REPAYMENT   ENERGIES   ENROLLED
COMBATING   MANFULLY   EXCAVATING   PERISHING
IDLENESS   MEROZ   LAZINESS   CRUCIBLE
DIAMOND   POLISHED   OPERATIONS   SAMSON

Morning

The LORD reigneth; let the earth rejoice.
—Psalm 97:1

There are no reasons for anxiety as long as today's blessed text is true. On earth, the Lord's power as readily controls the rage of the wicked as the rage of the sea. His love as easily refreshes the poor with mercy as the earth with showers. Majesty gleams in flashes of fire amid the tempest's horrors, and the glory of the Lord is seen in its grandeur in the fall of empires and the crash of thrones. In all our conflicts and tribulations, we may behold the hand of the divine King.

> God is God; He sees and hears
> All our troubles, all our tears.
> Soul, forget not, 'mid thy pains,
> God o'er all forever reigns.

In hell, evil spirits acknowledge, with misery, His undoubted supremacy. When they are permitted to roam abroad, it is with a chain at their heels. The bit is in the mouth of the behemoth, and the hook in the jaws of the leviathan. Death's darts are under the Lord's lock, and the grave's prisons have divine power as their warden. The terrible vengeance of the Judge of all the earth makes fiends cower and tremble, even as dogs fear the hunter's whip.

> Fear not death, nor Satan's thrusts,
> God defends who in Him trusts;
> Soul, remember, in thy pains,
> God o'er all forever reigns.

In heaven, none doubt the sovereignty of the King Eternal, but all fall on their faces to pay Him homage. Angels are His courtiers, the redeemed His favorites, and all delight to serve Him day and night. May we soon reach the city of the great King!

> For this life's long night of sadness
> He will give us peace and gladness.
> Soul, remember, in thy pains,
> God o'er all forever reigns.

```
D  I  P  Q  R  W  W  B  X  J  W  B  E  E  O  T  H  G  L  B
B  A  N  K  H  E  L  A  G  W  I  B  G  V  S  Z  O  S  J  T
V  O  N  O  M  L  A  H  R  S  C  B  L  D  T  K  U  W  P  O
K  N  M  X  B  A  B  D  T  D  K  K  E  Y  H  T  X  K  C  V
C  Z  D  L  I  W  F  F  I  N  E  K  A  T  R  F  Z  K  V  T
R  R  O  A  M  E  F  M  W  L  D  N  M  Q  U  G  U  R  X  W
H  I  B  P  G  D  T  B  D  S  Y  D  S  G  S  L  T  A  K  M
E  D  W  R  S  P  K  Y  C  P  Z  M  L  I  T  E  M  T  I  Z
E  L  D  W  U  M  F  A  T  P  B  B  P  B  S  I  J  U  M  L
C  Q  L  H  H  S  W  R  R  C  O  U  R  T  I  E  R  S  O  Z
G  A  C  K  N  O  W  L  E  D  G  E  C  Z  U  U  A  U  L  A
K  X  O  R  T  E  M  P  E  S  T  K  O  Y  G  J  S  H  M  A
C  E  K  W  Y  X  K  L  W  K  H  Y  N  H  R  U  H  P  Y  P
L  E  V  I  A  T  H  A  N  X  V  F  T  M  A  Z  G  A  L  H
T  R  I  B  U  L  A  T  I  O  N  S  R  C  G  C  J  I  O  P
C  H  S  J  Z  A  D  S  M  I  F  G  O  G  E  R  D  N  A  I
E  A  R  T  H  A  K  C  X  X  N  Q  L  W  H  F  D  S  J  H
F  L  A  S  H  E  S  E  O  P  F  E  S  R  E  I  G  N  S  T
R  R  T  Y  W  W  L  W  R  S  U  P  R  E  M  A  C  Y  G  V
R  R  J  D  B  B  E  H  E  M  O  T  H  S  T  C  N  W  C  I
```

ANXIETY	EARTH	READILY	CONTROLS
RAGE	WICKED	GLEAMS	FLASHES
TEMPEST	TRIBULATIONS	PAINS	ACKNOWLEDGE
SUPREMACY	ROAM	BEHEMOTH	LEVIATHAN
WARDEN	THRUSTS	REIGNS	COURTIERS

Evening

The bow shall be seen in the cloud.
—Genesis 9:14

The rainbow, the symbol of God's covenant with Noah, is a type of the Lord Jesus, who is God's witness to the people. When may we expect to see the sign of the covenant? The rainbow can only be seen painted against the backdrop of clouds. When a sinner's conscience is dark with clouds, when he remembers his past sin, mourns over it, and repents before God, Jesus Christ is revealed to him as the covenant Rainbow, displaying all the glorious colors of the divine character as a testimony to the sinner's peace with God. When a believer's trials and temptations surround him, it is sweet for him to think about the Lord Jesus Christ—to remember how He lived, bled, rose, and is even now interceding for His people. God's Rainbow is placed over the cloud of our sins, our sorrows, and our afflictions, to prophesy deliverance. A cloud alone does not produce a rainbow; there must also be raindrops to reflect the light of the sun. In the same way, sorrow for sin must not only threaten to fall on us, but must really fall on us, if we are to see God's Rainbow. Note that Christ would not have been our Redeemer if the vengeance of God had been merely a threatening cloud. Punishment had to fall in terrible drops upon our Surety. Until there is *real* anguish in the sinner's conscience, Christ cannot be his Savior. Until the conviction that the sinner experiences becomes grievous, he cannot see Jesus. But there must also be a sun, for clouds and drops of rain do not create rainbows unless the sun also shines. Beloved, our God, who is as the sun to us, always shines, but we do not always see Him—clouds hide His face. Yet no matter what drops may be falling or what clouds may be threatening, if He shines, there will be a rainbow at once. It is said that when we see a rainbow, the rain showers are over. Certainly, when Christ comes, our troubles leave. When we see Jesus, our sins vanish and our doubts and fears subside. When Jesus walks the waters of the sea, how profound the calm is!

```
Q U I A D J N Y R C D N I U N S P S Z I
Y H D J I G R M H V G K T Y F I I Z C I
F J R A S E S K U V L K H J P M V G T P
Y X R N P P S V D V O H R B R L F J N A
O V A G L O U O W Z B P E A O Y V O T I
A Z I U A A R R L A L R A C F Z T H D N
H L N I Y I R D O F K O T K O P E C H T
P W B S I J O E R X V P E D U X B E Q E
S C O H N J U S C R W H N R N A K X U D
N Y W B G H N M H F U E I O D O M T A U
X Q M P E N D A O N S S N P I W V E S Q
E V O B Y W G T L U C Y G X P I W S U T
N A H V O V H S A D R W L O T T V T R E
E Y O R U L Z U N Y E N Q I Z N R I E R
D I R F Q O K F T S W W S Z A E N M T R
Y G E P U N I S H M E N T Z K S R O Y I
J W K P V U K H D X E G H G C S Y N S B
A F F L I C T I O N S J P Q F U B Y S L
X B P H R W R E P E N T S G V V L K L E
R I Z C O L O R S V L Z R X S T X D T F
```

RAINBOW	SYMBOL	WITNESS	SIGN
PAINTED	BACKDROP	MOURNS	REPENTS
DISPLAYING	COLORS	TESTIMONY	SURROUND
AFFLICTIONS	PROPHESY	THREATENING	PUNISHMENT
TERRIBLE	SURETY	ANGUISH	PROFOUND

Morning

He hath commanded his covenant for ever.
—Psalm 111:9

The Lord's people delight in the covenant. It is an unfailing source of consolation to them as often as the Holy Spirit leads them into its banqueting house and waves its banner of love. They delight to contemplate the antiquity of that covenant, remembering that before the sun knew its place or planets followed their orbits, the interests of the saints were made secure in Christ Jesus. It is particularly pleasing to them to remember the sureness of the covenant, while meditating on *"the sure mercies of David"* (Isa. 55:3). They delight to celebrate it as signed, sealed, and ratified, in all things ordered well. It often makes their hearts swell with joy to think of its immutability, as a covenant that neither time nor eternity, life nor death, will ever be able to violate—a covenant as old as eternity and as everlasting as the Rock of ages. They rejoice also to feast on the fullness of this covenant, for they see in it all things provided for them. God is their portion, Christ their Companion, the Spirit their Comforter, earth their house, and heaven their home. They see in it an inheritance reserved and assigned to every soul possessing an interest in its ancient and eternal gift. Their eyes sparkled when they saw it as a gold mine in the Bible; but oh, how their souls were gladdened when they saw in the last will and testament of their divine Kinsman that it was bequeathed to them! More especially it is the pleasure of God's people to contemplate the graciousness of this covenant. They see that the law was made void because it was a covenant of works and depended on merit; but this they perceive to be enduring because grace is the basis, grace the condition, grace the strain, grace the bulwark, grace the foundation, grace the top-stone. The covenant is a treasury of wealth, a granary of food, a fountain of life, a storehouse of salvation, a charter of peace, and a haven of joy.

```
T L H N F U M N W D M E C R Z F E E F J
E K I N S M A N H S E W F U A L W D C W
S E C U R E E R K B D I O M Z L T W S D
S U R E N E S S O N I U L U G D J H J N
Y L D M D P U D U B T Q L I B R C A H B
H R C A A W C C L O A X O S E U S V B A
J C O N T E M P L A T E W N Q E T E R N
G Q F M L W B O U N I E E B U A D N Q Q
L A S S I G N E D T N Z D A E S T L O U
O E B X K Q B G H E G X I N A N A K W E
E C T X N R S A C F I T O V T H N J P T
U E J P E C B K C K P F J T H Z T E L I
V P Y M W Q H U Z Q Y C Z E E M I Q A N
J E P W Y J G K L A B D Z L D J Q U N G
Q W Q F R H S U A W U A C P A D U N E K
O R B I T S T U N F A I L I N G I N T H
O Q F S P A R K L E D R D W K Y T S S U
N E Z C H A R T E R Q P K Q X O Y Z J O
S F J E P A N C I E N T V U Q A G E S M
Z P F B J Y S Q S T O R E H O U S E K Z
```

UNFAILING	BANQUETING	CONTEMPLATE	ANTIQUITY
KNEW	PLANETS	FOLLOWED	ORBITS
SECURE	SURENESS	MEDITATING	ASSIGNED
ANCIENT	SPARKLED	KINSMAN	BEQUEATHED
BULWARK	STOREHOUSE	CHARTER	HAVEN

Evening

The people, when they beheld him, were greatly amazed,
and running to him saluted him.
—Mark 9:15

What a great difference there was between Moses and Jesus! After Moses had spent forty days with God on Mount Sinai, he underwent a kind of transfiguration, so that his face shone with great brightness. When he came down from the mountain, he put a veil over his face, for the people could not endure to look upon the glory. This was not the case with our Savior. He was transfigured with a greater glory than that of Moses. (See Mark 9:2–8.) Yet the Bible does not say that the people were blinded by the blaze of His countenance. Rather, they *were greatly amazed, and running to him saluted him.* The glory of the law repels, but the greater glory of Jesus attracts. Although Jesus is holy and just, so much truth and grace is blended with His purity that sinners run to Him, amazed at His goodness and fascinated by His love. They greet Him, become His disciples, and take Him as their Lord and Master. Reader, it may be that you are even now being blinded by the dazzling brightness of the law of God. You feel its claims on your conscience, but you cannot obey it in your life. It is not that you find fault with the law. On the contrary, it commands your most profound respect. Yet you are not drawn to God by it at all. Instead, your heart is hard, and you are close to desperation over it. Poor heart, turn your eyes from Moses, with all his repelling splendor, and look to Jesus, resplendent with gentler glories. See the blood flowing from His wounds and His head crowned with thorns! He is the Son of God; therefore, He is greater than Moses. Yet He is also the Lord of love and is more tender than the lawgiver. He bore the wrath of God. In His death, He revealed more of God's justice than Sinai did when it was ablaze with God's glory. However, God's justice has been vindicated, and now it is the guardian of believers in Jesus. Sinner, look to the bleeding Savior. As you feel the attraction of His love, run to His arms, and you will be saved.

```
Z H F C U N D E R W E N T D C G U E S M
V A M A Z E D P G S B P Y G V G E Y A V
Y E X Q J M O U N T L T F C Y M B D L I
H D C R L W O R Z K A C M I Z T M M U N
Q C L Y Z N K P D C Z Y W D I J B G T D
J S P Y X S U K T X E G I E N D U R E I
A S I Q O I X H L Y T E J D A D R W D C
T R A N S F I G U R A T I O N P R O C A
B G V D A A M O S E S D J Y L O K N F T
R N Y N N I M X S J C S N I H D D Y Y E
I Q Q N G I V J D S R S U B U L A Y M D
G C W M Q Z D B A G P K U L F H Z V S D
H B B L I N D E D N Q L M R J K Z I B Z
T P C J F A S C I N A T E D T J L J U F
N U Z G E X O N J Y Y O K N A Y I S L O
E U U V T C O N T R A R Y H D S N H E R
S I E X A P P S R N J P X H L O G O Y T
S M Z M G U A R D I A N U Q W I R N V Y
I A V F B N I C C Z G C P T S R F E P F
U N A T T R A C T I O N D B P V C L L F
```

MOSES	FORTY	MOUNT	SINAI
UNDERWENT	TRANSFIGURATION	SHONE	BRIGHTNESS
ENDURE	BLINDED	BLAZE	AMAZED
SALUTED	FASCINATED	DAZZLING	CONTRARY
SPLENDOR	VINDICATED	GUARDIAN	ATTRACTION

Morning

Thou shalt guide me with thy counsel,
and afterward receive me to glory.
—Psalm 73:24

The psalmist felt his need of divine guidance. He had just been discovering the foolishness of his own heart, and lest he would be constantly led astray by it, he resolved that God's counsel would henceforth guide him. A sense of our own folly is a great step toward being wise, when it leads us to rely on the wisdom of the Lord. The blind man leans on his friend's arm and reaches home in safety. Likewise, we should give ourselves up implicitly to divine guidance, nothing doubting, assured that though we cannot see, it is always safe to trust the all-seeing God. *"Thou shalt"* is a blessed expression of confidence. He was sure that the Lord would not decline the condescending task. There is a word for you, believer; rest in it. Be assured that your God will be your counselor and friend. He will guide you and will direct all your ways. In His written Word you have this assurance in part fulfilled, for Holy Scripture is His counsel to you. We are happy to have God's Word always to guide us! What would the mariner be without his compass? And what would the Christian be without the Bible? This is the unerring chart, the map in which every shoal is described, and all the channels from the quicksands of destruction to the haven of salvation are mapped and marked by One who knows all the way. Bless You, O God, that we may trust You to guide us now, and guide us even to the end! After this guidance through life, the psalmist anticipated a divine reception at last—*"and afterward receive me to glory."* What a thought for you, believer! God Himself will receive you to glory—you! Though you are wandering, erring, straying, yet He will bring you safe at last to glory! This is your portion. Live on it this day, and if perplexities should surround you, go, in the strength of this text, straight to the throne.

```
D Z E G C A N T I C I P A T E D J T I Q
E Z W N H H Y A C A A T J Q L V X Z M E
S M D V A M L Z H D N F X L T A W N P S
T R E H R W S V A E V G E B T T S L L C
R O C I T X F W N V N T U J H D G S I R
U T L V E Q W Q N T L C E I A F Q A C I
C P I B X L I K E W I S E D D D G M I P
T B N I Z Z A B L C I N G F W A H B T T
I P E V P K U H S D F R W Y O Z N N L U
O D R F P J C H Q F V O T E J R O C Y R
N X E E Z V S Y E M J C K R N R T C E E
V E D I S C O V E R I N G R K N S H H G
T P E R P L E X I T I E S I A B O V R O
U E C O U N S E L L V U U N F B Z R Z J
X E Q A U M A R I N E R G G L C W F Y P
K K B Y O A T F G Y Y R E S O L V E D N
A H F Q Q S K D L S S W E B X N K L C C
A E F O O L I S H N E S S T E H R K J B
O D O U B T I N G V P C O M P A S S O C
S T R A Y I N G R L W B T P G Y B P P Q
```

GUIDANCE	DISCOVERING	FOOLISHNESS	RESOLVED
COUNSEL	HENCEFORTH	LIKEWISE	IMPLICITLY
DOUBTING	DECLINE	SCRIPTURE	MARINER
COMPASS	CHART	CHANNELS	DESTRUCTION
ANTICIPATED	ERRING	STRAYING	PERPLEXITIES

Evening

Trust in him at all times.
—Psalm 62:8

Faith is as much the rule of temporal life as it is of spiritual life. We ought to have faith in God for our earthly matters as well as for our heavenly concerns. It is only as we learn to trust in God to supply all our daily needs that we will live above the world. We are not to be idle, for that would show that we do not trust in God, who continually works, but in the devil, who is the father of idleness. We are not to be imprudent or rash, for that would be to trust chance rather than the living God, who is a God of economy and order. Acting in all prudence and uprightness, we are to rely simply and entirely on the Lord at all times. Let me commend to you a life of trusting in God in temporal things. By trusting in God, you will not have to repent for having used sinful means to grow rich. Serve God with integrity. If you achieve no success, at least no sin will be on your conscience. By trusting in God, you will not become guilty of self-contradiction. He who trusts only in his own abilities sails this way today and that way the next, like a boat tossed about by the fickle wind. However, he who trusts in the Lord is like a steamship, which cuts through the waves, defies the wind, and makes one bright, silvery, straightforward track to her desired haven. Be someone who has living principles within him. Never yield to the varying practices of worldly wisdom. Walk in the path of integrity with determined steps, and show that you are invincibly strong in the strength that confidence in God alone can provide. Thus you will be delivered from burdensome care. You will not be troubled by bad news. Your heart will be steadfast, *"trusting in the* LORD*"* (Ps. 112:7). How pleasant it is to float along the stream of providence! There is no more blessed way of living than living a life of dependence upon a covenant-keeping God. We have no cares, *"for he careth for* [us]*"* (1 Pet. 5:7). We have no troubles, because we cast our burdens upon the Lord.

```
N E I S B C A H J J M Q F V U W F Z I L
O Z A U E P O N F P J B G A V I X Z M Y
Y S Q R S U J M Y L B U G R I Z H U P I
B A C A T N M E M B O V V D Q T E F R E
R I O Q W H S Y E U A J G O K H I U X
G L A M H R L I B P N R T O N A A C D S
F S R N V W X Y N Q D D W Z K V K E I
H I U P R I G H T N E S S E I S Y L N L
B B Q O D K F N E R D W J R N J D E T V
T D D E P E N D E N C E F U V S G M W E
T B H S T R A I G H T F O R W A R D S R
K G F H G K R F E G B Z U F S J U P F Y
P A G K Z D T E M P O R A L W A V E S C
D D S W L T C A X Z Z S N H D S Y X S N
Z C O N C E R N S B V O M A W P D O Z S
V Y T I N V I N C I B L Y X A G E V G X
S C G L P T X X W B L B S M Y F D C L Y
C X R A S H I R Y M A T T E R S Y M C V
L V C M R E C O N O M Y U J O A U F G M
K I A C C K E R S T E A M S H I P P A P
```

FAITH   TEMPORAL   EARTHLY   MATTERS
CONCERNS   IMPRUDENT   RASH   ECONOMY
UPRIGHTNESS   COMMEND   SAILS   FICKLE
STEAMSHIP   WAVES   SILVERY   STRAIGHTFORWARD
INVINCIBLY   FLOAT   DEPENDENCE   BURDENS

Morning

I will; be thou clean.
—Mark 1:41

Primeval darkness heard the Almighty command, *"Let there be light"* (Gen. 1:3), and immediately *"there was light"* (v. 3). The word of the Lord Jesus is equal in majesty to that ancient word of power. Redemption, like Creation, has its word of might. Jesus speaks, and it is done. Leprosy yielded to no human remedies, but it fled at once at the Lord's *"I will."* The disease exhibited no hopeful signs or tokens of recovery. Nature contributed nothing to its own healing, but the unaided word effected the entire work on the spot and forever. The sinner is in a plight more miserable than the leper. Let him imitate the leper's example and go to Jesus, *"beseeching him, and kneeling down to him"* (Mark 1:40). Let him exercise what little faith he has, even though it should go no further than, "Lord, *'if thou wilt, thou canst make me clean'* (v. 40)." There need be no doubt as to the result of the application. Jesus heals all who come and casts out none. In reading the narrative in which our morning's text occurs, it is worthy of devout notice that Jesus touched the leper. This unclean person had broken through the regulations of the ceremonial law and pressed into the house, but Jesus, far from chiding him, broke through the law Himself in order to meet him. Jesus made an interchange with the leper, for while He cleansed him, He contracted by that touch a Levitical defilement. Likewise, Jesus Christ was made sin for us, although in Himself He knew no sin, so that we might be made the righteousness of God in Him. Oh, that poor sinners would go to Jesus, believing in the power of His blessed substitutionary work, and they would soon learn the power of His gracious touch. That hand that multiplied the loaves, that saved sinking Peter, that upholds afflicted saints, that crowns believers, that same hand will touch every seeking sinner and in a moment make him clean. The love of Jesus is the source of salvation. He loves, He looks, He touches us, and we live!

```
D E F I L E M E N T Q P Y S N H A X L E
G U V I Z F L T F G Z J L U K O A C L Q
O F Y H K K D G R X U N A I D E D D O J
Z S R I J G A L M I G H T Y G M E N A K
Z W Z E H S Y N T L G F E N N H E G V T
H V V P M B E B D F E L I S A L T D E M
H C H K N E E L I N G P B A T T A A S J
H G P B I Z D Y W S C F R H A K U J F D
C A M T S P P I F Y R Q N O U F G R V E
P L Z Z I Q M E E Q C S K M S N J M E V
U E R D N U O V L S V E F Q T Y R K G O
K V P C K J P R I M E V A L Z O H D I U
N I D Q I B B A C D C Z F C C U B X U T
C T R S N H R S F W V L B F Y B C J P G
B I W B G E J I M M E D I A T E L Y H P
C C Q P H B Z I S J A H J J R A S Z O A
D A R E D E M P T I O N G D L M P A L A
Y L B E S E E C H I N G P E T E R F D P
Q C X N M U L T I P L I E D A Z N T S S
S U B S T I T U T I O N A R Y S U P U Y
```

PRIMEVAL	ALMIGHTY	IMMEDIATELY	REDEMPTION
LEPROSY	REMEDIES	NATURE	UNAIDED
PLIGHT	BESEECHING	KNEELING	DEVOUT
LEVITICAL	DEFILEMENT	SUBSTITUTIONARY	MULTIPLIED
LOAVES	SINKING	PETER	UPHOLDS

Evening

Just balances, just weights, a just ephah, and a just hin, shall ye have.
—Leviticus 19:36

Weights, scales, and measures are all to be set according to the standard of justice. Surely, no Christian needs to be reminded of this in his business, for if righteousness were banished from the rest of the world, it would find shelter in believing hearts. There are, however, other balances that weigh moral and spiritual things, and these often need examining. Are the balances in which we weigh our own and others' characters accurate? Do we not turn our own ounces of goodness into pounds, and other people's bushels of excellence into pecks? Pay attention to weights and measures, Christian. Are the scales in which we measure our trials and troubles according to standard? Paul, who suffered more than we do, called his afflictions *"light"* (2 Cor. 4:17). Yet we often think that our afflictions are heavy. Surely, something must be amiss with the weights! We must see to this matter, lest we be reported to the heavenly court for unjust dealing. Are the weights with which we measure our doctrinal beliefs fair? The doctrines of grace should have the same weight with us as the precepts of the Word—no more and no less. However, it is to be feared that, with many people, one scale or the other is unfairly weighted. It is important to give a just measure in truth. Christian, be careful in regard to this. The measures by which we estimate our obligations and responsibilities look rather small. When a rich man contributes no more to the cause of God than a poor man contributes, is that *"a just ephah, and a just hin"*? When min-isters are half starved because of our selfishness, is that honest dealing? When the poor are despised while ungodly rich men are held in admiration, is that a just balance? Reader, I might lengthen the list, but I prefer to leave it as your evening's work to discover and destroy all unrighteous balances, weights, and measures in your life.

```
I Q S T A N D A R D P P N W N J N S O E
F D O R M O R A L J Z T B B B I F J K Y
K O F P E E L J U I X H S U N J U S T X
G L G U D G X H F N J X B C S R W U E F
Q B J P W U A A O R G K X S A H O I D R
G X Q E F G Z R M X M O T E H L E N H U
B F M C V I C H D I B X D M A R E L Z A
K R I K D F S M D H N O O L I Q C S S P
R A N S R Y J P K E Z I S Q Y P A U Z O
K D S Q V V O B M Q A R N Y U Y R P S U
C O N T R I B U T E S L J G U B E A W N
X Q F D E S P I S E D Q I A Q I F G T D
K W J Q G P L W I D D J P N B P U O X S
B Y S H T W H B P J Y O B N G K L U K B
Y O Y Y I P A U N F A I R L Y W Y N E L
R E S P O N S I B I L I T I E S A C J N
A W R K A G W L H I I G Y Q V V R E D N
W Y Q P K O Q A B R T P L G P Q V S U L
A W E I G H T E D U H X S T V R P W Z X
A A C C O R D I N G B A L A N C E S M Z
```

SCALES   ACCORDING   STANDARD   BALANCES

MORAL   EXAMINING   OUNCES   POUNDS

BUSHELS   PECKS   UNJUST   DEALING

UNFAIRLY   WEIGHTED   CAREFUL   REGARD

RESPONSIBILITIES   CONTRIBUTES   DESPISED   UNGODLY

Morning

The sword of the LORD, and of Gideon.
—Judges 7:20

Gideon ordered his men to do two things. Covering up a torch in an earthen pitcher, he told them, at an appointed signal, to break the pitcher and let the light shine. Then they were to sound the trumpet, crying, *"The sword of the LORD, and of Gideon!"* This is precisely what all Christians must do. First, you must shine; break the pitcher that conceals your light. Throw aside the bushel that has been hiding your candle and shine. Let your light shine before men; let your good works be such that, when men look on you, they will know that you have been with Jesus. Then there must be the sound, the blowing of the trumpet. There must be active exertions for the ingathering of sinners by proclaiming Christ crucified. Take the Gospel to them. Carry it to their door. Put it in their way. Do not allow them to escape it; blow the trumpet right against their ears. Remember that the true war cry of the church is Gideon's watchword, *"The sword of the LORD, and of Gideon!"* God must do it; it is His own work. But we are not to be idle. Instrumentality is to be used—*"The sword of the LORD, and of Gideon!"* If we only cry, *"The sword of the LORD!"* we will be guilty of an idle presumption; and if we shout, *"The sword of Gideon!"* alone, we will manifest idolatrous reliance on an arm of flesh: we must blend the two in practical harmony, *"The sword of the LORD, and of Gideon!"* We can do nothing of ourselves, but we can do everything by the help of our God. Let us, therefore, in His name determine to go out personally and serve with our flaming torch of holy example and with our trumpet tones of earnest declaration and testimony. God will be with us, our enemy will be put to confusion, and the Lord of Hosts will reign forever and ever.

```
W I K W Y L Y Q E J R V I O J J N O D K
Z S T Z Z E H P A V C A N D L E I O Z M
O O T M P H V R R Q B A S J I W D A V V
L U R S I Z Y O T Z K M T N D C O J Y B
W N U O T F H C H F E Q R E P K L M D D
C D M E C O Y L E E A A U D K Z A O J C
O L P E H C J A N Y C B M O M C T N D A
N D E C E W P I U I C Z E J O L R W E R
C X T E R A U M G D D H N M U P O S C R
E E B L X I X I G Y K I T K O S U I O Y
A H X U S E L N B A F D A J J H S Z V F
L U R Y A I R G K L U I L R M T Q E E L
S V T Y F Z C T M E R N I S W O R D R A
I N G A T H E R I N G G T J Z B Z U I M
X W Q E U A K C L O N V Y F T N X Q N I
V J M G T O K X Q S N L H S R O E N G N
A X T L G I D E O N F S C D O G R X T G
G A J D K A S H G A L Q C H P V Q C N I
C W I P S X O R D E R E D K E Q F X H O
R D D U P R E C I S E L Y W X I K V S T
```

GIDEON	ORDERED	COVERING	TORCH
EARTHEN	PITCHER	SOUND	TRUMPET
SWORD	PRECISELY	CONCEALS	HIDING
CANDLE	EXERTIONS	INGATHERING	PROCLAIMING
CARRY	INSTRUMENTALITY	IDOLATROUS	FLAMING

Evening

In the evening withhold not thine hand.
—Ecclesiastes 11:6

Opportunities are plentiful in the evening. People return to their homes after work, and the zealous soulwinner finds time to go about telling of the love of Jesus. Am I engaged in evening work for Jesus? If not, let me no longer withhold my hand from a service that requires abundant labor. Sinners are perishing for lack of knowledge. He who delays may find the hems of his clothes crimson with the blood of souls. (See Jeremiah 2:34.) Jesus submitted both of His hands to the nails when He died on the cross. How can I keep back one of mine from His blessed work? Night and day, He toiled and prayed for me. How can I give a single hour to pampering my flesh with luxurious ease? Get up, idle heart. Stretch out your hands to work, or lift them up in prayer. Heaven and hell are in earnest. Let me be earnest, also, and sow good seed this evening for the Lord my God. The evening of life also has a claim on us. Life is so short that a morning of humanity's vigor and an evening of decline are the sum of it. To some people, life seems long, but a nickel is a great sum of money to a poor man. Life is so brief that no one can afford to lose a day. It has been well said that if a great king were to present us with a huge pile of gold and tell us to take as much of it as we could count in a day, we would make a long day of it. We would begin early in the morning and not stop even when it was evening. Winning souls is a far nobler work. Then why do we withdraw from it so soon? Some people are spared for a long evening of vigorous old age. If that is the case with me, let me use the talents that I still retain and serve my blessed and faithful Lord to my last hour. By His grace, I will die in the harness. I will lay down my charge only when I lay down my body. Those who are elderly may instruct the young, comfort the fainthearted, and encourage the despondent. If evening has less vigorous heat, it should have more calm wisdom. Therefore, in the evening, I will not withhold my hand.

```
V I G O R O U S H C E E Y D D H G K P N
F V P L F F M L P I J C V D N O G S A A
P W I M O O E P I X T L Y E M S G T M G
V O L G T I L R W P C O K I N P J Y P K
G Q V U O E I Z P S H T V H C I O A E N
L P Y N X R L D A A H S U O Z N R R F
Z L V Q I U H L A B Y E I H L S T G I A
V S Y O S G R M I N U S C L Z X H J N I
B Q Z R U Z X I C N I N U I U R Q E G N
X U Z N P B D S O R G C D K Q F Z R E T
Q I B M H G F D J U Z B K A I G G E N H
Y D H A R N E S S V S C Z E N B L M C E
I C K L G A S U U E I R S E L T H I O A
F F Z K P Z Y O J W Q E V K I B D A U R
T A C I J L R L B Z Y T R S S P W H R T
I Q H E M S U K E N L A E O X W E F A E
A P L E N T I F U L N I Q A G T U X G D
S O U L W I N N E R T N P R S N B D E X
J D E S P O N D E N T P W C A E A J Z W
D B P H V T T A L E N T S L D Q W C U B
```

PLENTIFUL	EVENING	SOULWINNER	TELLING
ABUNDANT	HEMS	CLOTHES	JEREMIAH
PAMPERING	LUXURIOUS	EASE	VIGOR
NICKEL	VIGOROUS	TALENTS	RETAIN
HARNESS	FAINTHEARTED	ENCOURAGE	DESPONDENT

Morning

I saw by night, and behold a man riding upon a red horse, and he stood among the myrtle trees that were in the bottom.
—Zechariah 1:8

The vision in this chapter describes the condition of Israel in Zechariah's day. Being interpreted in its aspect toward us, it describes the church of God as we find it now in the world. The church is compared to a myrtle grove flourishing in a valley. It is hidden, unobserved, secret. It courts no honor and attracts no observation from the careless gazer. The church, like her Head, has a glory, but it is concealed from carnal eyes, for the time of her breaking forth in all her splendor is not yet come. The idea of tranquil security is also suggested to us, for the myrtle grove in the valley is still and calm, while the storm sweeps over the mountain summits. Tempests spend their force on the craggy peaks of the Alps, but down where the stream flows that makes glad the city of our God, the myrtles flourish by the still waters, all unshaken by the impetuous wind. How great is the inward tranquility of God's church! Even when opposed and persecuted, she has a peace that the world does not give, and which, therefore, it cannot take away. The peace of God that passes all understanding keeps the hearts and minds of God's people. Does not the metaphor forcibly picture the peaceful, perpetual growth of the saints? The myrtle sheds not its leaves; it is always green. And the church, in her worst time, still has a blessed verdure of grace about her; in fact, she has sometimes exhibited the healthiest growth when her winter has been sharpest. She has prospered most when her adversities have been the most severe. Hence the text hints at victory. The myrtle is the symbol of peace and a significant token of triumph. The brows of conquerors were bound with myrtle and with laurel. Is not the church always victorious? Are not Christians *"more than conquerors"* (Rom. 8:37) through Christ who loves them? Living in peace, do not the saints fall asleep in the arms of victory?

```
C C H A P T E R Q O D Y V D O E G B R D
A O O H P Z H G R O W T H N M Q W W C W
X R N I U J Q E I T P T T O Y M H P B L
M E C D A J C A X E P E F Y Q Z E S G N
Q H F V I C O L A U R E L X B I A Q U I
Q E U I N T E R P R E T E D D C L E N V
A D V E R S I T I E S H E F S R T E O E
O I G E J G R O H B J B J R Z A H B B R
C X Q B X Q H N N N H N X L F P G I I S D
C O Z E C H A R I A H I F U M G E C E U
A G M G A B Q V W H M H H P M Y S R R R
R H R P J E Q C W M K Y X I H M T D V E
E J A O A C R M G I S P R W D S I O E W
L A B A V R Q L T Y R R B T M D Y Z D A
E S T Q Q E E D W H M B E T L K E G H G
S L S M X V Y D T C P M S H S E A N H U
S K B N Y F L O U R I S H I N G I U G H
R I T W F L Q I N R X G K T Z I R A G V
O W D C I D X Z T D J Q A S P E C T M Z
V O A V I S I O N D E S C R I B E S Y O
```

VISION	CHAPTER	DESCRIBES	CONDITION
ZECHARIAH	INTERPRETED	ASPECT	COMPARED
MYRTLE	GROVE	FLOURISHING	HIDDEN
UNOBSERVED	CARELESS	CRAGGY	VERDURE
HEALTHIEST	GROWTH	ADVERSITIES	LAUREL

Evening

Howl, fir tree, for the cedar is fallen.
—Zechariah 11:2

When the crash of a falling oak is heard in the forest, it is a sign that the woodsman is at work. Every tree in the forest may tremble, for fear that tomorrow the sharp edge of the ax will find it out. We are all like trees marked for the ax. The fall of one should remind us that, whether we are as great as the cedar or as humble as the fir, the appointed hour is quickly creeping up on every one of us. I trust that we have not become callous toward death by hearing about it often. May we never be like the birds in the church steeple, which build their nests when the funeral bells are tolling and sleep quietly when the solemn peals are startling the air. May we regard death as the weightiest of all events and be sobered by its approach. It is foolish to spend our time on frivolous matters while our eternal destiny hangs on a thread. The sword is out of its sheath—let us not trifle with it. The sword is polished, and the edge is sharp— let us not play with it. He who does not prepare for death is more than an ordinary fool; he is a madman. When the voice of God is heard among the trees of the garden, let fig tree, sycamore, elm, and cedar alike hear the sound of it. Be ready, servant of Christ, for your Master comes without delay. He will come when an ungodly world least expects Him. See to it that you are faithful in His work, for a grave will soon be dug for you. Be ready, parents. See to it that your children are brought up in the fear of God, for they will soon be without their fathers and mothers. Be ready, you who are engaged in business. Make sure that your affairs are in order and that you serve God with all your hearts. The days of your earthly service will soon be over, and you will be called to give account for what you did while in the body, whether good or evil. May we all prepare for the tribunal of the great King with a circumspection that will be rewarded with the gracious commendation, *"Well done, good and faithful servant"* (Matt. 25:23).

```
Q C N A S G E E N Y J W R F D F Z B Y M
Y R U C L N D P V W H I G L P Y U V H D
S E W A O W Z H V L R E O C E G F L U T
D E T L K Q A P M Y N D Q M A W E J I R
F P I L S W F Z Z Q B L R A L J Q I S I
F I R O H U N O W J U V L T S C U B N B
I N N U Q I A L R V Z I N T M M A V K U
X G K S F L F E H E I U C H Z Q P Z Y N
H F M L W E D K A I S U N K G A P K H A
U U F S M A D M A N Y T N P L K O K O L
E N F T L Z B F M A P H X J F Y I H A G
D E D D U K C Q M U W F Q E G K N R K C
G R R K D E S T I N Y M C H S P T M M Q
E A X C A N S T E E P L E I Y L E E R B
Y L A X Q T E I T C W J Q W P A D P I I
T B U C X T B P F N J B O D F O H A B R
O M M W C I R C U M S P E C T I O N S D
S H A R P B V C R A S H X Q L C I S V S
N O Y T H R E A D C A W O O D S M A N Q
C N M A S Y C A M O R E W J N E F F G X
```

CRASH	OAK	FOREST	WOODSMAN
SHARP	EDGE	APPOINTED	QUICKLY
CREEPING	CALLOUS	BIRDS	STEEPLE
FUNERAL	PEALS	DESTINY	THREAD
MADMAN	SYCAMORE	TRIBUNAL	CIRCUMSPECTION

Morning

Pleasant fruits, new and old, which I have
laid up for thee, O my beloved.
—Song of Solomon 7:13

The spouse desires to give all that she produces to Jesus. Our hearts have "*all manner of pleasant fruits*" (Song 7:13) both "*new and old,*" and they are laid up for our Beloved. At this rich autumn season of fruit, let us survey our harvest. We have "*new*" fruits. We desire to feel new life, new joy, new gratitude. We wish to make new resolves and carry them out by new labors. Our hearts blossom with new prayers, and our souls pledge themselves to new efforts. But we have some "*old*" fruits, too. There is our first love. What a choice fruit! Jesus delights in it. There is our first faith. It is the simple faith by which, having nothing, we became possessors of all things. There is our joy when first we knew the Lord; let us revive it. We have our old remembrances of the promises. How faithful God has been! In sickness, how softly He made our beds! In deep waters, how placidly He lifted us up! In the flaming furnace, how graciously He delivered us. Old fruits, indeed! We have many of them, for His mercies have been more than the hairs of our heads. Old sins we must regret, but then we have had times of repentance that He has given us, by which we have wept our way to the cross and learned the merit of His blood. We have fruits, this morning, both new and old; but here is the point—they are all laid up for Jesus. Truly, those are the best and most acceptable services in which Jesus is the solitary aim of the soul, and His glory, without any addition whatever, is the end of all our efforts. Let our many fruits be laid up only for our Beloved. Let us display them when He is with us and not hold them up before the gaze of men. Jesus, we will turn the key in our garden door, and none will enter to rob You of one good fruit from the soil that You have watered with Your bloody sweat. Our all will be Yours, Yours only, O Jesus, our Beloved!

```
N U M A S M O R Y M K P L Y H A V H C N
R B A D M D Z D H A I R S D L O Q T H B
S A N C E B Q P L A C I D L Y J J C O S
I U N Q A L A Q Z S E J R F Y I A M I P
T T E S Y L I L J K I Q S B H J V K C O
O U R B I S G V R A D W W X A B A E E U
R M X J U C T F E Y O K J A R D C E P S
F N I P U O K O Z R Y R B T V N C K I E
V S U R V E Y N W Z E V L R E X E P J V
E Q K S Y I D O E P R D O V S I P S I H
Q N P B Z G W M M S D M S U T E T I P C
X T R L B X M M W S S X S S V L A M L T
F X O Y U N L X E E M G O E E J B P E H
L C D A T C Y A P X B P M U G N L L D Y
B R U N V C K Z T W D L B Z S M E E G G
O V C B T W B T H E M S E L V E S S E S
Y N E R H I W K U K G R A T I T U D E F
S P S B F M K W V Z P J S X V L W V P Y
F Y J J G S O L O M O N Q N E B E Q G A
H E A D S R C K U P A H I Q E U N D Y K
```

SOLOMON	SPOUSE	PRODUCES	MANNER
AUTUMN	SURVEY	HARVEST	GRATITUDE
BLOSSOM	PLEDGE	THEMSELVES	CHOICE
SIMPLE	SICKNESS	PLACIDLY	DELIVERED
HAIRS	HEADS	WEPT	ACCEPTABLE

Evening

The LORD will give grace and glory.
—Psalm 84:11

It is the nature of Jehovah to be bounteous. He delights in giving. His gifts are precious beyond measure and are as freely given as the light of the sun. He gives grace to His elect because He wills it, to His redeemed because of His covenant, to the called because of His promise, to believers because they seek it, to sinners because they need it. He gives grace abundantly, seasonably, constantly, readily, sovereignly—doubly enhancing the value of the blessing by the way in which He gives it. He freely gives grace, in all its forms, to His people. He generously and unceasingly pours into their souls comforting, preserving, sanctifying, directing, instructing, and assisting grace. He will always give grace bountifully, no matter what may happen to us. We may become sick, but the Lord will give grace. We may experience poverty, but grace will surely be provided. Death must come, but grace will light a candle at the darkest hour. Reader, how blessed it is, as the seasons come and go, and as the leaves begin to fall again, to enjoy such an unfading promise as this: *"The LORD will give grace and glory."* The little conjunction *"and"* in this verse is a diamond rivet that binds the present with the future, for grace and glory always go together. God has married them, and no one can divorce them. The Lord will never deny glory to someone when He has freely granted that person the right to live in His grace. Indeed, glory is nothing more than grace in its Sunday best, grace in full bloom, grace like autumn fruit—ripe and perfected. No one can tell how soon we may have glory! It may be that before this month of October has ended, we will see the Holy City. However, whether the interval is long or short, we will be glorified before long. The Lord will surely give glory to His chosen—the glory of heaven, the glory of eternity, the glory of Jesus, the glory of the Father. Glory is the exceptional promise of a faithful God!

Two golden links of one divine chain:

Who owns grace will surely glory gain.

```
F K D P P B M A E M Z U I T H R A C W A
R T G F D E G B X B N E U Y B Z X O Y A
E H O O I Z I U C P A R L M E C I N D I
E S M R V M V N E K J S I Z Y J P J M L
L Z S M O J E D P B Q P Y O O U A U I D
Y T C S R Z S A T E G D M Q N A E N N T
A A N C C G M N I B C O U J D R O C S S
B P C P E R D T O L A O T D E U G T T E
I W L Q F J U L N B A D P R L N G I R A
Y O R D H B R Y A S U N D A Y F M O U S
W M C C E Z C J L N A I R U I A T N C O
N H D T A I R R O A V A L U E D O L T N
Y A O E O E C C G Z S W B D H I V F I A
Q E X Y S B H S S D T H E B R N G F N B
T X J A V E E L I Y O U U Y E G Q K G L
D C K S V N C R U N C E A S I N G L Y Y
J O T Q L D Q H G I F T S Q A W A X Z S
Q E N H A N C I N G A M F H A N T Q S S
H K C A L L E D F B O U N T E O U S M H
X D Y D I R E C T I N G Q W K C D A Z C
```

BOUNTEOUS	GIFTS	BEYOND	FREELY
GIVES	CALLED	ABUNDANTLY	SEASONABLY
ENHANCING	VALUE	FORMS	UNCEASINGLY
DIRECTING	INSTRUCTING	UNFADING	CONJUNCTION
DIVORCE	SUNDAY	OCTOBER	EXCEPTIONAL

155

Morning

Are they not all ministering spirits, sent forth to minister for
them who shall be heirs of salvation?
—Hebrews 1:14

Angels are the unseen attendants of the saints of God. They bear us up in their hands, lest we dash our foot against a stone. Loyalty to their Lord leads them to take a deep interest in the children of His love. They rejoice over the return of the Prodigal to his father's house below, and they welcome the advent of the believer to the King's palace above. In olden times, the sons of God were favored with their visible appearance, and at this day, although unseen by us, heaven is still opened, and the angels of God ascend and descend on the Son of Man so that they may visit the heirs of salvation. Seraphim still fly with live coals from off the altar to touch the lips of men who are greatly beloved. If our eyes could be opened, we would see horses and chariots of fire around the servants of the Lord; for we have come to an innumerable company of angels, who are all watchers and protectors of the royal seed. Edmund Spenser's line is no poetic fiction, where he sings,

How oft do they with golden pinions cleave
 The flitting skies, like flying pursuivant
Against foul fiends to aid us militant!

To what dignity are the chosen elevated when the brilliant courtiers of heaven become their willing servants! Into what communion are we raised since we have fellowship with spotless celestials! How well are we defended since all the twenty thousand chariots of God are armed for our deliverance! To whom do we owe all this? Let the Lord Jesus Christ be forever endeared to us, for through Him we are made to sit *in heavenly places* (Eph. 2:6) far above principalities and powers. He it is whose camp is *round about them that fear him* (Ps. 34:7). He is the true Michael whose foot is on the dragon. All hail, Jesus! To You, the Angel of Jehovah's presence, this family offers its morning vows.

```
Z Q L R R D X K I I K P C L E A V E O F
D R A G O N I Y H V I V P G R D S J E H
L R C U I F G L A F U N S U C T T E N B
U O U J N W E L C O M E O E H N Z O A S
C Z Y Z X S P O I H U Z S O A T U B H T
T O Q A B I E B T A E P M C R Q V P F B
E Z A I L B B E I C D R J D I J K R D M
Y E J L P T B D N M H O P X O X S O B O
F O K E S B Y E V I K D S S T Q U T I V
V T N F T A F I Q C A I I O S Y I E N C
F J F L Y S P U W H K G N B X D L C N Q
K W I H U C I E M A Y A M K A Q X T U P
Q A E E R E K O A E N L U G D W A O M I
C T N A Q N K E Y L A C R L A H F R E N
J C D G S D B Y L H K F T K O P Y S R I
T H S W A T T E N D A N T S L N A J A O
S E R A P H I M R V I M A V D V Y U B N
V R R C L P N R I E X O W Z E M P T L S
V S Q R V B H P E H E F X D N N P E E K
Z I M I L I T A N T T O I F O U L D Z C
```

UNSEEN	ATTENDANTS	LOYALTY	PRODIGAL
WELCOME	OLDEN	ASCEND	SERAPHIM
COALS	CHARIOTS	INNUMERABLE	WATCHERS
PROTECTORS	PINIONS	CLEAVE	FOUL
FIENDS	MILITANT	MICHAEL	DRAGON

Evening

He himself hath suffered being tempted.
—Hebrews 2:18

This is a well-known concept, yet it tastes sweet to the weary heart: Jesus was tempted in the same ways I am. You probably have heard this truth many times, but have you really grasped it? He was tempted to commit the very same sins into which we fall. Do not disassociate Jesus from our common humanity. You are going through a dark place, but Jesus has already gone through it. You are waging a fierce battle, but Jesus has stood toe-to-toe with the same enemy. Let us be encouraged. Christ carried the load before we did, and the bloodstained footsteps of the King of Glory may be seen along the road that we are now traveling. Yet there is something even sweeter than the knowledge that Jesus was tempted in the same way that we are: although Jesus was tempted, He never sinned; therefore, it is not necessary for us to sin. Jesus was a man, and if one Man endured these temptations and did not sin, then in His power, the members of His body may also refrain from sin. Some who are just beginning the Christian life think that they cannot be tempted without sinning. However, they are mistaken. There is no sin in *being* tempted, only in *yielding* to temptation. This truth is comforting for those who are being severely tempted. There is still more to encourage them if they will reflect on the fact that the Lord Jesus, though tempted, gloriously triumphed. As He overcame, His followers will also surely overcome, for Jesus is the representative Man for His people. The Head has triumphed, and the members share in the victory. Fears are needless, for Christ is with us, armed for our defense. Our place of safety is in the Savior. Perhaps we are being tempted right now in order to drive us nearer to Him. Blessed is any wind that blows us into the port of our Savior's love! Blessed are the wounds that make us seek the beloved Physician. You who are tempted, come to your tempted Savior. He can sympathize with your weaknesses. He will come to the aid of everyone who is tried and tempted.

```
P H S E G V V W C O N C E P T P I P Y H
E A O E C B M R M X Z L H J R H L P J F
A T N O J H W C R M L B M E N Y Q A D O
I H W A G I N G D F Q L V C A S J U H O
A V E S N T A S T E S O S G C I G F E T
Y L M R R M G Y E M V O V C L C T B B S
Q U N R G B M R V J E D C W Z I R O R T
X G R A S P E D U L I S Z Z B A A S E E
T F O L L O W E R S B T G U I N V Y W P
N Z S T V D O H Y E D A P A J O E M S S
E L Q L E N K E H T P I D Q B D L P B J
E E H H U M A N I T Y N B D B G I A N E
D A E M B S P K F G X E B M I J N T M E
L J I A G D W T Y I P D Z U E B G H A L
E K P S T N D R E E O V Z Z N R N I K A
S N S O E J M T G D C N A Y P H X Z S B
S C P R E F R A I N Y S U F F E R E D I
P R O B A B L Y C J W D C Y G N E V X U
W O V F G L F Q G L O R I O U S L Y Y V
G Q D I S A S S O C I A T E F R G N S R
```

HATH	SUFFERED	TEMPTED	HEBREWS
CONCEPT	TASTES	PROBABLY	GRASPED
DISASSOCIATE	HUMANITY	WAGING	BLOODSTAINED
FOOTSTEPS	TRAVELING	REFRAIN	GLORIOUSLY
FOLLOWERS	NEEDLESS	PHYSICIAN	SYMPATHIZE

Morning

*He arose, and did eat and drink, and went in the strength of that
meat forty days and forty nights.*
—1 Kings 19:8

All the strength supplied to us by our gracious God is meant for service, not for wantonness or boasting. When the prophet Elijah found the cake baked on the coals and the cruse of water placed at his head as he lay under the juniper tree, he was no gentleman to be gratified with dainty fare so that he might stretch himself at his ease; far from it. He was commissioned to go forty days and forty nights in the strength of it, journeying toward Horeb, the mount of God. When the Master invited the disciples to *"come and dine"* (John 21:12) with Him, after the feast was concluded, He said to Peter, *"Feed my sheep"* (vv. 16–17). He further said, *"Follow me"* (v. 19). This is true with us also. We eat the bread of heaven so that we may expend our strength in the Master's service. We come to the Passover and eat of the Paschal Lamb with loins girded and staff in hand, so as to start off at once when we have satisfied our hunger. Some Christians are for living *on* Christ, but are not so anxious to live *for* Christ. Earth should be a preparation for heaven, and heaven is the place where saints feast most and work most. They sit down at the table of our Lord, and they serve Him day and night in His temple. They eat of heavenly food and give perfect service. Believer, in the strength you daily gain from Christ, labor for Him. Some of us have yet to learn much concerning the design of our Lord in giving us His grace. We are not to retain the precious grains of truth as the Egyptian mummy held the wheat for ages, without giving it an opportunity to grow. We must sow it and water it. Why does the Lord send down the rain on the thirsty earth and give the genial sunshine? Is it not that these may all help the fruits of the earth to yield food for man? Even so, the Lord feeds and refreshes our souls so that afterward we may use our renewed strength in the promotion of His glory.

```
A T R U V P X L U I Q F K M W T E W D T
B L O I N S S J E K U L N K A W J G R E
T Y M G M W W C R U S E Y K N U W R I M
F G Z Y O U L E T S W V E A T J B A N M
N Y E K S G S P E T C F C A O E A T K R
X B X G D U F A Y R L R O R N U P I E C
X Y L M G F P D H E L C M M N T X F G S
G I R D E D A H K T R A M F E O G I Y P
H B P E C R S O J C E K I O S E M E P C
U D O Z D R C R U H U E S Z S Z C D T G
J V X A B I H O N X W H S U M T P A I E
Q W O Z S W A M I F J Y I M U M M Y A N
E R Z B Z T L S P X H M O Y L Q Y G N T
A L K W G W I C E E E M N A L A M B M L
W A I X O S L N R M A I E W V R H O Q E
G W O J F W E U G W U G D E R Q I Q G M
Z D E Q A M K O R S S E V A M Z U Z O A
O L L F I H S E N A N B Q B X X W G P N
T A X M E A T E B A K E D F R E K V C I
V V B O K H O R E B M A Z R C M H L V G
```

DRINK	MEAT	WANTONNESS	BOASTING
ELIJAH	CAKE	BAKED	CRUSE
JUNIPER	GENTLEMAN	GRATIFIED	STRETCH
COMMISSIONED	HOREB	PASCHAL	LAMB
LOINS	GIRDED	EGYPTIAN	MUMMY

Evening

He that believeth and is baptized shall be saved.
—Mark 16:16

Mr. MacDonald asked the inhabitants of the island of St. Kilda, Scotland, how a person must be saved. An old man replied, "We will be saved if we repent, forsake our sins, and turn to God." "Yes," said a middle-aged woman, "and with a true heart, too." "Aye," rejoined a third, "and with prayer." A fourth added, "It must be the prayer of the heart." "And we must be diligent, too," said a fifth, "in keeping the commandments." Each having contributed his thoughts, and feeling that a very decent creed had been put together, they all looked to the preacher and waited for his approval—but they had aroused his deepest pity. The carnal mind always maps out for itself a way in which self can work and become great. However, the Lord's way is quite the reverse. Believing and being baptized are not matters of merit to be gloried in. They are so simple that boasting is excluded. It is God's free grace that has won the victory. It may be that you are unsaved. If so, what is the reason? Do you think that the way of salvation prescribed in the text is doubtful? How can that be, when God has pledged His own Word for its certainty? Do you think it is too easy? Then why do you not obey it? Its ease leaves those who neglect it without excuse. To believe is simply to trust, to depend, to rely on Christ Jesus. To be baptized is to submit to the ordinance that our Lord fulfilled at the Jordan River (see Matthew 3:13–17), that the converted ones submitted to at Pentecost (see Acts 2:1–42), and that the jailer yielded obedience to on the very night of his conversion (see Acts 16:23–33). Baptism is an outward sign of inward faith. It does not save, but it demonstrates to us our death, burial, and resurrection with Jesus. Like the Lord's Supper, it is not to be neglected. Do you believe in Jesus? Then, dear friend, dismiss your fears, for you will be saved. Are you still an unbeliever? Then remember that there is only one Door. (See John 10:7–9.) If you will not enter by it, you will perish in your sins.

```
L F I R L I H B W J S H G Y H U R T T J
L S X A O E V T N K I L D A N N V S H P
L G C X C U Q D E V I X V M H S Q U M R
G Z B O M Y K O O V N Q I J U A H P Y E
I S A C T V D N V Z H E R A N V N P Z S
W N P J U L J M I Q A J E R B E Y E D C
S D T N N N A M Y E B Q S O E D P R U R
R X I I Y W R N I L I O U U L R P V W I
Y A Z G S K C P D D T X R S I M E P D B
H P E N T E C O S T A G R E E X X U E E
J V D I S M I S S J N T E D V G C J C D
Q I Z X A I Q T L J T Z C K E U L L E D
T Y P R H E Y C M T S X T F R X U Y N C
K Q U N S K X N O N D U I O S J D W T T
E F K W K V B C J P P I O E W I E Y T I
B J A I L E R H U R O O N E B O D D S B
T X H Z U T B X D S T Y J O R D A N Z Y
O Q F B Q Y Z C R E E D K V W C P P S G
S D U M A C D O N A L D K Q E O C E S T
D D W L M T A P P R O V A L G L W K L B
```

BAPTIZED   MACDONALD   INHABITANTS   KILDA
SCOTLAND   DECENT   CREED   APPROVAL
AROUSED   EXCLUDED   UNSAVED   PRESCRIBED
EXCUSE   JORDAN   PENTECOST   JAILER
RESURRECTION   SUPPER   DISMISS   UNBELIEVER

Morning

Thy paths drop fatness.
—Psalm 65:11

Many are *"the paths of the Lord"* (Ps. 25:10) that *"drop fatness,"* but a special one is the path of prayer. No believer who spends much time in prayer will have any need to cry, *"My leanness, my leanness, woe unto me!"* (Isa. 24:16). Starving souls live at a distance from the mercy seat and become like parched fields in times of drought. Prevalence with God in wrestling prayer is sure to make the believer strong—if not happy. The nearest place to the gate of heaven is the throne of heavenly grace. Spend much time alone with Jesus, and you will have much assurance; spend little time alone with Him, and your religion will be shallow, polluted with many doubts and fears, not sparkling with the joy of the Lord. Since the soul-enriching path of prayer is open to the very weakest saint; since no high attainments are required; since you are not bidden to come because you are an advanced saint, but freely invited if you are a saint at all; see to it, dear reader, that you are often in the place of private devotion. Spend much time on your knees, for so Elijah drew the rain down on famished Israel's fields. There is another special path dripping with fatness to those who walk therein: it is the secret walk of communion. Oh, the delights of fellowship with Jesus! Earth has no words that can set forth the holy calm of a soul leaning on Jesus' breast. Few Christians understand it. They live in the lowlands and seldom climb to the mountaintop. They live in the outer court. They do not enter the holy place. They do not take up the privilege of priesthood. At a distance they see the sacrifice, but they do not sit down with the priest to eat of it and to enjoy the fat of the burnt offering. But, reader, always sit under the shadow of Jesus. Come up to that palm tree and take hold of the branches of it. Let your Beloved be to you as the apple tree in the woods, and you will be satisfied as with marrow and fatness. Jesus, visit us with Your salvation!

```
A P X F S C C J T D I X Z H W S G T N W
T S A C N R Y F P E F N I A U R S N M E
T D Z L V N D U X Q C K V N X N W M A A
A I H E M N E A R E S T X I A H T V R K
I Z F V S G U Z N I K M A E T W C K R E
N E N R I C H I N G I E D J H E A P O S
M D H D K J D J R Q Z K M A P C D O W T
E X E I S D R I P P I N G S C T E L E Q
N Q W V P S C I Z J R H M K C M X L H L
T H S K O R P J T F N D P J P G D U W O
S O O T E T E T B A A B B R R D R T R W
Z S P P U A I V I S X T Q I H S O E E L
O N T Y B J O O A D S S N X D D P D S A
U F N A I P X Q N L G R N E T D V X T N
A A F X R V K D N L E W H S L E J L D
J P J C P V F S R X M N G N Y S B N I S
B D P P D M I I H E C Z C N X Y X F N F
P L W L L E A N N E S S G E I M V I G N
W G G W E S P O G C A O B X F Q Y H I G
V J J J F H U M O U N T A I N T O P F S
```

DROP	FATNESS	LEANNESS	STARVING
PREVALENCE	WRESTLING	NEAREST	POLLUTED
ENRICHING	WEAKEST	ATTAINMENTS	BIDDEN
INVITED	DEVOTION	DRIPPING	LOWLANDS
MOUNTAINTOP	PALM	APPLE	MARROW

Evening

Behold, to obey is better than sacrifice.
—1 Samuel 15:22

Saul had been commanded to slay all the Amalekites and their cattle. Instead of doing so, he preserved the king and allowed the Israelites to take the best of the oxen and sheep. When called to account for this, he declared that he had done it with the idea of offering sacrifices to God. However, Samuel immediately countered him with this certain truth: sacrifices are no excuse for an act of direct rebellion. The text for this evening is worthy to be printed in letters of gold, and to be hung up before the eyes of the present idolatrous generation. They are very fond of the fineries of worshipping their own wills, yet they utterly neglect the laws of God. Always remember that to keep strictly in the path of your Savior's commands is better than any outward form of religion. Listening to His precepts with an attentive ear is better than bringing the *"fat of rams"* (1 Sam. 15:22), or any other precious thing, to place on His altar. If you are failing to keep the least of Christ's commands to His disciples, I urge you not to be disobedient any longer. All the pretensions you make of attachment to your Master, and all the devout actions that you may perform, are no recompense for disobedience. *"To obey,"* even in the slightest thing, *"is better than sacrifice"*—no matter how elaborate it is. We are not to rely on Gregorian chant, sumptuous robes, incense, or banners in our desire to please God. The first thing that God requires of His child is obedience. Even though you might give your body to be burned, and all your goods to feed the poor, if you do not listen to the Lord's precepts, all your formalities will be of no profit to you. It is a blessed thing to be as teachable as a little child. However, it is a much more blessed thing, when one has been taught the lesson, to carry it out to the letter. How many people decorate their churches and adorn their clergymen, but refuse to obey the Word of the Lord! Do not be like one of them.

```
K T E X E I A C T N C Q N D E F D S Q R
M E J Q C H A N T A F O A J B V I A H E
J A C M G C L R R F Q R M L Q T S M J C
O C G C R E G H P E Y H Y M C E O U Y O
T H X F E L X H P E G C Q J A I B E N M
R A E N G A N A Q D D R A B V N E L E P
S B M N O B L I E K M C B I Q F D D L E
N L D Z R O V R Q D E F I N E R I E S N
D E C K I R C O U N T E R E D K E C D S
C I Q V A A A P R E C E P T S F N O K E
G U S L N T H L X E M R A B B V T R A L
H B L R C E O H L C I P Z G M U F A L B
T J A O W X J H Y A K T C W C L T T Y L
L X Y U S F N Z Z R G I M Q B L A E O S
S Y R J A D O R N H S U M P T U O U S A
R J E Z J W V H W S B E K D L X K E P U
O B E Y V C D V P R E T E N S I O N S L
W F F F O R M A L I T I E S Q U U V O J
F B M D H G H U S R X I T X S F R L S G
A T T A C H M E N T D Q X V X C Q Q Q T
```

OBEY SAMUEL SAUL COMMANDED
SLAY COUNTERED FINERIES DISOBEDIENT
PRETENSIONS ATTACHMENT RECOMPENSE ELABORATE
GREGORIAN CHANT SUMPTUOUS PRECEPTS
FORMALITIES TEACHABLE DECORATE ADORN

Morning

It is a faithful saying.
—2 Timothy 2:11

Paul had four of these "*faithful*" sayings. The first occurs in 1 Timothy 1:15, "*This is a faithful saying, and worthy of all acceptation, that Christ Jesus came into the world to save sinners.*" The next is in 1 Timothy 4:8–9, "*Godliness is profitable unto all things, having promise of the life that now is, and of that which is to come. This is a faithful saying and worthy of all acceptation.*" The third is in 2 Timothy 2:11–12, "*It is a faithful saying:… If we suffer, we shall also reign with him.*" The fourth is in Titus 3:8, "*This is a faithful saying,…that they which have believed in God might be careful to maintain good works.*" We may trace a connection among these faithful sayings. The first one lays the foundation of our eternal salvation in the free grace of God, as shown to us in the mission of the great Redeemer. The next affirms the double blessedness that we obtain through this salvation—the blessings of the upper and lower springs—of time and of eternity. The third shows one of the duties to which the chosen people are called. We are ordained to suffer for Christ with the promise that "*if we suffer, we shall also reign with him*" (2 Tim. 2:12). The last sets forth the active form of Christian service, bidding us to diligently maintain good works. Thus we have the root of salvation in free grace; next, the privileges of that salvation in the life which now is, and in that which is to come; and we also have the two great branches of suffering with Christ and serving with Christ, loaded with the fruits of the Spirit. Treasure up these faithful sayings. Let them be the guides of your life, your comfort, and your instruction. The apostle of the Gentiles proved them to be faithful; they are faithful still. Not one word will fall to the ground. They are worthy of acceptance. Let us accept them now and prove their faithfulness. Let these four faithful sayings be written on the four corners of your house.

```
J V R X A S U T X K Q A P A H P A U L X
M A I N T A I N V F A I T H F U L U M L
U H Y I I Z C S J C G X P C G O L R E Z
I G B M D I B U P H O E X S N Y Y E Q T
K N Y T H T Y F W U D G U Z F C L K F I
A D S A G C K F C U L G E N T I L E S M
Y J S T P H E E Q V I O X S N B C R J O
W G I Y R O T R E A N E D W Y L O W L T
I O R C W U S D U R E K U W H E N B K H
D V R X I E C T D I S Z U E W S N S B Y
B O Y T E M Z T L K S S P S H S E A J N
G W U A H D A M I E T H P T K E C Y V S
G L M B H Y O I J O S Q E V D D T I N P
D W S X L V V S F F N K R Q A N I N V L
V A E X A E P S U M R H O K G E O G G O
T Y A R D G P I N I Z R H O P S N Q D W
T R A C E K Y O F W Y J A J F S Q P O E
L Q Y X K J N N R H A O L G X N F V V R
Y U A C C E P T A T I O N T K Y X F Y A
T I T U S A F R J Z S L C P I J U I X C
```

PAUL   TIMOTHY   FAITHFUL   SAYING
ACCEPTATION   GODLINESS   WORTHY   SUFFER
TITUS   MAINTAIN   TRACE   CONNECTION
MISSION   DOUBLE   BLESSEDNESS   UPPER
LOWER   INSTRUCTION   APOSTLE   GENTILES

Evening

We are all as an unclean thing.
—Isaiah 64:6

The believer is a new creation. He belongs to a holy generation, a special people. The Spirit of God is in him, and, in all respects, he is far removed from the natural man. Yet, for all that, the Christian is still a sinner. He is a sinner because of the imperfection of his nature, and will continue to be so to the end of his earthly life. The blackened fingers of sin leave smudges on our whitest robes. Sin mars our repentance before the great Potter has finished it on the wheel. Selfishness defiles our tears, and unbelief tampers with our faith. The best thing we ever did independent of the merit of Jesus only swelled the number of our sins. For even when we have been purest in our own sight, we, like the heavens, have not been pure in God's sight. (See Job 15:15.) Since He charged His angels with folly, how much more must He charge us with it, even in our most angelic frames of mind. The song that ascends to heaven and seeks to emulate angelic tunes has human discords in it. The prayer that moves the arm of God is still a bruised and battered prayer, and only moves His arm because the sinless One, the great Mediator, has stepped in to take away the sin of our supplication. The most golden faith or the purest degree of sanctification that a Christian ever attained on earth still has so much alloy in it that it is only worthy of the flames, considered in itself. Every night that we look in the mirror, we see a sinner, and we need to confess, *"We are all as an unclean thing, and all our righteousnesses are as filthy rags"* (Isa. 64:6). Oh, how precious the blood of Christ is to hearts such as ours! How priceless a gift His perfect righteousness is! How bright our hope of perfect holiness in the next world is! Although sin dwells in us, even now, its power is broken; it has no dominion. It is like a broken-backed snake. We are in bitter conflict with it, but we are dealing with a vanquished enemy. In a little while, we will enter victoriously into the city where nothing defiles. (See Revelation 21:27.)

```
R Q Y D O M I N I O N Y T R X Y C P B H
G E S X P L N F F E A W S P Q S H R R J
U W W U N I H F R M M H C M C Q Y Z D D
Z E I K N N Q L B R G U X Y U Z Y J Y I
U W S N A K E Q T U G F L F L D H J H S
F R A M E S Z Q M E M G I A L J G X J C
M M Y B X Q C G Y U P H N B T R G E F O
I D S S H K V R M A H P D Q W E C M S R
R U B L A C K E N E D H E X L S T E I D
R N A O T F E F E I I S P N X P A F S S
O C T U L I C J W H I T E S T E M I A E
R L A H Z D M Q O U S F N H C C P L I I
S E L F I S H N E S S F D Q V T E T A H
Z A K N K T I D X Z J W E C G S R H H G
K N Q R D L A Q I X X V N A B I S Y G E
Q V A V Q M B S J Q U H T F I G L W B E
V A N Q U I S H E D H Q J C H T D A V G
N G Z Q I M P E R F E C T I O N M X P P
O A D C E Y B A T T E R E D W D G G X G
M L X T D E J L U Q V Y F I N G E R S K
```

UNCLEAN	ISAIAH	RESPECTS	IMPERFECTION
BLACKENED	FINGERS	SMUDGES	WHITEST
SELFISHNESS	TAMPERS	INDEPENDENT	FRAMES
EMULATE	DISCORDS	BATTERED	MIRROR
FILTHY	DOMINION	SNAKE	VANQUISHED

Morning

The church in thy house.
—Philemon 2

Is there a church in your house? Are parents, children, and friends all members of it, or are some still unconverted? Let us pause here and let the question be asked of each one: Am I a member of the church in this house? How a father's heart would leap for joy and a mother's eyes fill with holy tears if all were saved from the eldest to the youngest! Let us pray for this great mercy until the Lord grants it to us. Probably it had been the dearest object of Philemon's desires to have all his household saved, but it was not at first granted him in its fullness. He had a wicked servant, Onesimus, who, having wronged him, ran away from his service. His master's prayers followed him, though, and, at last, as God would have it, Onesimus was led to hear Paul preach. His heart was touched, and he returned to Philemon, not only to be a faithful servant, but a beloved brother, adding another member to the church in Philemon's house. Is there an unconverted member of the household absent this morning? Make special supplication that such may, on his return home, gladden all hearts with good news of what grace has done! Is there an unconverted person present? Let him partake in the same earnest entreaty. If there is such a church in your house, order it well, and let all act as in the sight of God. Move in the common affairs of life with studied holiness, diligence, kindness, and integrity. More is expected of a church than of an ordinary household. Family worship must, in such a case, be heartier and more devout. Internal love must be warmer and unbroken, and external conduct must be more sanctified and Christlike. We do not need to fear that the smallness of our number will remove us from the list of churches, for the Holy Spirit has here enrolled a family-church in the inspired book of remembrance. As a church, let us now draw near to the great Head of the one universal church, and let us ask Him to give us grace to shine before men to the glory of His name.

```
S U B B L X O R U T Q C S E P P N J T A
O N E S I M U S Z X C T U F Z H S O X F
A C D S U S L K W J V H P Z O I Q R M F
D O F N M E P J H R T F P G J L E D J A
T N U F J N I D O Q Q E L N F E X I P I
N V L T A T S M G U P D I V K M T N K R
C E L W K R H P Q E V M C U O O E A A S
C R N P R E A C H S U K A Q V N R R O Q
U T E L A A R B Z T F W T T A S N Y P T
N E S G T T Y X T I C W I O W X A Y A R
B D S Y R Y P W Q O I K O D C B L Y U M
R N U V A H A I J N N Z N W E T J O S V
O K J Z Z H O U S E H O L D L I N U E L
K V K E M U X K C X F M R F D A L N B L
E B M V V C O N D U C T C N E V F G V O
N G C S E R V A N T P D X S S Q W E Y E
B D R M E M B E R S V T P J H M S E S
U N I V E R S A L T U M D H E W C T V A
Q Y X I D P P B Z G E F I K X L A T C Z
L V Q I G D X B L I V L E R N M F J M H
```

PHILEMON	MEMBERS	UNCONVERTED	PAUSE
QUESTION	ELDEST	YOUNGEST	HOUSEHOLD
FULLNESS	SERVANT	ONESIMUS	PREACH
SUPPLICATION	ENTREATY	AFFAIRS	ORDINARY
UNBROKEN	EXTERNAL	CONDUCT	UNIVERSAL

Evening

And knew not until the flood came, and took them all away;
so shall also the coming of the Son of man be.
—Matthew 24:39

The doom was universal. Neither rich nor poor escaped. The learned and the illiterate, the admired and the hated, the religious and the profane, the old and the young, all sank in one common ruin. Some had undoubtedly ridiculed the patriarch Noah. Where are their lighthearted jests now? Others had threatened him for his zeal, which they had considered madness. Where are their boasting and harsh words now? The critic who judged the old man's work was drowned in the same sea that covered his sneering companions. Those who spoke patronizingly of the good man's faithfulness to his convictions, but did not share in them, sank to rise no more. All the workers who had helped to build the wondrous ark for pay were also lost. The flood swept them all away; it did not make a single exception. Similarly, for those who are outside of Christ, final destruction is sure. No rank, possession, or character will suffice to save a single soul who has not believed in the Lord Jesus. My soul, take note of this widespread judgment, and tremble at it. The general apathy of the people was astonishing! They were all *"eating and drinking, marrying and giving in marriage"* (Matt. 24:38), until the terrible morning dawned. There was not one wise man on earth outside the ark. Folly duped the whole race, folly in regard to self-preservation—the most foolish of all follies; folly in doubting the true God—the most malignant of foolishness. It is strange, is it not? All men are negligent of their souls until grace gives them reason. Then they leave their madness and act like rational beings—but not until then. May God be blessed, for all who were in the ark were safe. No ruin entered there. From the huge elephant down to the tiny mouse, all were safe. The timid hare was equally as secure as the courageous lion; the helpless coney was as safe as the industrious ox. Everyone who is in Jesus is safe. Are you in Him this evening?

```
L L T I B I Y V N T U P U C O O R K T B
K R V Y C N M K H U S W N B Y L E M T L
A D G M R D G Y A U X O D T I F L A V C
Z E F A I U B W E A P D O O H H I K Z F
U R L D T S M N F N A I U O O T G N A M
J Z O N I T I W R B T L B O C M I E M O
E C O E C R N I S X R L T J E N O H P U
S Q D S E I C D A G O I E V T R U J R S
T V U S S O P S U O N T D F K M S W O E
S M N H B U U P B L I E L L B W T O F C
P M B X Z S U R P L Z R Y Y M O H D A G
O Q F G I Q P E R K I A M H M S A C N S
S L T R R W A A A D N T S R I K F T E N
P F G C J R I D C F G E L H M J M G H E
N X P M M J M I J H L L X W A S B A L E
C F K A D M I R E D Y K J C U R D C V R
P L I G H T H E A R T E D N V D E G O I
Z Q Q N S V O U A B U O I S W O W V E N
G N L H L I P A T R I A R C H T W H O G
M U H A P A T H Y E L E P H A N T D C H
```

FLOOD	DOOM	ILLITERATE	ADMIRED
RELIGIOUS	PROFANE	UNDOUBTEDLY	PATRIARCH
LIGHTHEARTED	JESTS	MADNESS	CRITIC
SNEERING	PATRONIZINGLY	WIDESPREAD	APATHY
ELEPHANT	MOUSE	HARE	INDUSTRIOUS

Morning

I will pour water upon him that is thirsty.
—Isaiah 44:3

When a believer has fallen into a low, sad state of feeling, he often tries to lift himself out of it by chastening himself with dark and doleful fears. This is not the way to rise from the dust, but to continue in it. You might as well chain the eagle's wing to make it mount as to doubt in order to increase your grace. It is not the law, but the Gospel that saves the seeking soul at first; and it is not a legal bondage, but gospel liberty that can restore the fainting believer afterward. Slavish fear does not bring the backslider back to God, but the sweet wooings of love allure him to Jesus' bosom. Are you thirsting for the living God this morning and unhappy because you cannot find Him to the delight of your heart? Have you lost the joy of religion, and is this your prayer, *"Restore unto me the joy of thy salvation"* (Ps. 51:12)? Are you conscious also that you are barren like the dry ground and that you are not bringing forth the *"fruit unto God"* (Rom. 7:4) that He has a right to expect of you? Are you aware that you are not as useful in the church or in the world as your heart desires to be? Then here is exactly the promise that you need, *"I will pour water upon him that is thirsty."* You will receive the grace you so much require, and you will have it to the utmost extent of your needs. Water refreshes the thirsty: you will be refreshed, and your desires will be gratified. Water quickens sleeping vegetable life; your life will be quickened by fresh grace. Water swells the buds and makes the fruits ripen; you will have grace that will make you fruitful in the ways of God. Whatever good quality there is in divine grace, you will enjoy it to the full. All the riches of divine grace you will receive in abundance. You will be, as it were, drenched with it. As sometimes the meadows become flooded by the bursting rivers and the fields are turned into pools, so will you be; the thirsty land will be transformed into springs of water.

```
L I B E R T Y N T G B H Q U A L I T Y C
D A Q V W D P D E P Y D P W J S S S Z N
R W G Q K P W C H A S T E N I N G R T D
Y G I C W Y U U M I F B B H M R U C A H
E S U E S O Q G T T X U T M E M X N F D
A C M I G I E Z K M J Q X C A G V O X R
G T F F U H N F J N O O R P D H R Q B E
L C B K U C E C U N D S Z P O V R A P N
E A R A V I J X R J E Q T C W E N L O C
B U R S T I N G A E X S B B S G K L S H
F A I N T I N G B C A J V V U E B U L E
N E W F E M M O I D T S H L T T C R E D
A Y F R G N X W W D I L E P L A U E E A
J Y H U Y B R M M L W J Y B F B B B F P W
O I Y I S P Y J P D S F Q I D L G E I Y
D X I T J W O O I N G S S X H E A A N T
Z O L F G J M X D O L E F U L J C R G Q
S D W U Q X H C G P J R N X K P Z S V C
T G J L T R A N S F O R M E D I Z Z G V
X I G K M P W G F E K W E X T E N T V V
```

CHASTENING	DOLEFUL	FEARS	EAGLE
INCREASE	LIBERTY	FAINTING	WOOINGS
ALLURE	EXACTLY	UTMOST	EXTENT
SLEEPING	VEGETABLE	FRUITFUL	QUALITY
DRENCHED	MEADOWS	BURSTING	TRANSFORMED

Evening

*This is the blood of the testament which God
hath enjoined unto you.*
—Hebrews 9:20

There is a strange power about the word *blood,* and the sight of it is always affecting. A kind heart cannot bear to see a sparrow bleed, and unless it has become accustomed to it, it turns away with horror at the slaughter of an animal. As for the blood of men, it is a consecrated thing. It is murder to shed it in wrath, and it is a terrible crime to squander it in war. Is the reason for this solemnity the fact that *"the blood is the life"* (Deut. 12:23), and that the pouring out of blood is a sign of death? I think so. When we contemplate the blood of the Son of God, our awe is increased even more, and we shudder when we think of the guilt of sin and the terrible penalty that the Sin-bearer endured. Blood, always precious, is priceless when it streams from Immanuel's side. The blood of Jesus seals the covenant of grace and makes it forever sure. Covenants of old were made by sacrifice, and the everlasting covenant was ratified in the same manner. Oh, the delight of being saved on the sure foundation of divine pledges that cannot be dishonored! Salvation by the works of the law is a frail and broken vessel whose ship-wreck is sure. However, the covenant vessel fears no storms, for the blood insures that it will stay intact. The blood of Jesus made His testament valid. Wills have no power unless the testators die. In this light, the soldier's spear that pierced the Savior's side is a blessed aid to faith, since it proved that our Lord was really dead. There can be no doubt about that matter; therefore, we may boldly take hold of the legacies He has left for His people. Happy are those who see their title to heavenly blessings assured them by a dying Savior. But does this blood have nothing to say to us? Does it not call us to sanctify ourselves to Him by whom we have been redeemed? Does it not call us to *"newness of life"* (Rom. 6:4) and stir us to entire consecration to the Lord? Oh, that the power of the blood might be known and felt in us this night!

```
E Q W I T P H A M J B D Z X J V X H R X
F Z X C L R O Y O B E N J O I N E D H C
M V X O C I R V D L R N K K E A U R O O
E U N N P C R T E S T A M E N T H A T N
N I S S B E O J B K I X X H G J N Q M S
X Z I E T L R T Q P N K K H V M R A W E
W S G C Y E O R O P E F D P K Y H N T C
X G H R E S M H S P A N K S U Y H I Z R
L E T A T S U N H I O A A Y P J A M W A
T E F T I S Y U I X Q R A L U H C A Y T
G Q X I K Y P Z P M D X T A T I C L L E
O Y L O Z O E A W L V J F C Q Y U S N D
F J L N U V F D R M O E B T T K S Q E C
X S T O R M S E E R T W L L T A T U W H
P T R J T G N E C V O H D E L C O A N N
B Q L R Q J X D K G B W V D H Z M N E R
X S X J B H R E S U W X J E T U E D S A
C R I M E S H U D D E R C S U G D E S W
O A F F E C T I N G K L S Y Y D W R J J
F T Z P M M U R D E R L E G A C I E S G
```

TESTAMENT	ENJOINED	SIGHT	AFFECTING
SPARROW	ACCUSTOMED	HORROR	ANIMAL
CONSECRATED	MURDER	CRIME	SQUANDER
SHUDDER	PENALTY	PRICELESS	SHIPWRECK
STORMS	LEGACIES	NEWNESS	CONSECRATION

Morning

I will cut off the remnant of Baal from this place, and…
them that worship the host of heaven upon the housetops;
and them that swear by the LORD, and that swear by Malcham.
—Zephaniah 1:4-5

Such persons thought themselves safe because they were with both parties. They went with the followers of Jehovah and bowed at the same time to Malcham. But duplicity is abominable with God, and His soul hates hypocrisy. The idolater who distinctly gives himself to his false god has one sin less than he who brings his polluted and detestable sacrifice to the temple of the Lord while his heart is with the world and the sins thereof. To hold with the hare and run with the hounds is a coward's policy. In the common matters of daily life, a double-minded man is despised, but in religion he is loathsome to the last degree. The penalty pronounced in the verse before us is terrible, but it is well deserved. How should divine justice spare the sinner, who knows the right, approves it, and professes to follow it, and all the while loves evil and gives it dominion in his heart? My soul, search yourself this morning, and see whether you are guilty of double-dealing. You profess to be a follower of Jesus, but do you truly love Him? Is your heart right with God? Are you of the family of old Father Honest, or are you a relative of Mr. Stretch-the-Truth? A good name is of little value if I am indeed dead in trespasses and sins. To have one foot on the land of truth and another on the sea of falsehood will involve a terrible fall and total ruin. Christ will be all or nothing. God fills the whole universe; therefore, there is no room for another god. If He reigns in my heart, there will be no space for another reigning power. Do I rest alone on Jesus crucified and live alone for Him? Is it my desire to do so? Is my heart set on doing so? Then, blessed be the mighty grace that has led me to salvation. If this is not the case, O Lord, pardon my sad offense and unite my heart to fear Your name.

```
K J W F Q D M J Y R J Y H D R U Y I B U
W Y A O Z L W A B E L O A T H S O M E N
Z D C I F X Q E L A U R C X C H I B L I
Q E E Y C F K D Q C A H E D B X S F D V
B T P S J X E Z D A H L K I R H D Q W E
X B Z H E C G N D K S A M S L A E C Z R
C F X L A R Z P S W T M M T G L T Q I S
O D A B D N V K X E H R C I R I E K Y E
D K U L L I E A C E P K N A D S G N Y
L O R P S U K A D H R A L C P O T S R A
B C E X L E Q C H Q E R T L W L A D T K
T N L I G I H M P Q O E J Y U A B B M Q
C A A H K W C O S X F M P L C T L B H W
E Y T Z O G G I O W F N J O M E E P B H
R Z I Y P N A B T D P A F H E R E L Z O
W I V U V U E N H Y T N R A J E N U A U
U V E M Q Z A S K K P T C Y L G V V V N
Y Y G Y S Q U M T T L V M C R S C T W D
R T J W A P K C K G K A I C R A E I K S
F M P O L I C Y L L C O W A R D B S G B
```

REMNANT	BAAL	MALCHAM	ZEPHANIAH
DUPLICITY	IDOLATER	DISTINCTLY	FALSE
DETESTABLE	THEREOF	HOUNDS	COWARD
POLICY	LOATHSOME	DESERVED	HONEST
RELATIVE	FALSEHOOD	UNIVERSE	OFFENSE

Evening

And Laban said, It must not be so done in our country,
to give the younger before the firstborn.
—Genesis 29:26

We do not excuse Laban for his dishonesty, but we do not hesitate to learn from the custom that he quoted as his excuse. There are some things that must be taken in order, and if we want to gain the second, we must secure the first. The second may be more lovely in our eyes, but the rule of the heavenly country must stand, and the elder must be married first. For instance, many believers desire the *"beautiful and well favoured"* (Gen. 29:17) Rachel of *"joy and peace in believing"* (Rom. 15:13), but they must first be wedded to the *"tender eyed"* (Gen. 29:17) Leah of repentance. Everyone falls in love with happiness, and many would cheerfully serve twice seven years to enjoy it. However, according to the rule of the Lord's kingdom, the Leah of real holiness must be beloved to our souls before the Rachel of true happiness can be attained. Heaven does not come first but second, and only by persevering to the end can we gain a share in it. The cross must be carried before the crown can be worn. We must follow our Lord in His humiliation, or we will never rest with Him in glory. My soul, are you so vain as to hope to break through the heavenly rule? Do you hope for reward without labor, or honor without toil? Dismiss that idle expectation, and be content to take the difficult things for the sake of the sweet love of Jesus, which will compensate you for everything. In such a spirit, laboring and suffering, you will find that bitter things grow sweet, and hard things easy. Like Jacob, your years of service will seem to you but a few days, because of the love you have for Jesus. Then, when the dear hour of the Wedding Feast has come, all your toils will be as though they had never been. An hour with Jesus will make up for ages of pain and labor.

Jesus, to win Yourself so fair,
    Your cross I will with gladness bear:
Since so the rules of heaven ordain,
    The first I'll wed the next to gain.

```
B N Y D B M T C E B G H L L E P M X R Q
B K N V J B P Z W X M B A A V Y W G A W
E Y E D U Z W S T P N J D B E O J M L L
H P E X P E C T A T I O N A R H G L L E
Q O J M C W W V N U L R U N Y T R G X A
U F L G O V M E Q V D E P X O S K S E H
O N H I U I A W D C O M P E N S A T E J
T R C B N G J I Y D E B H F E O E I Y D
E F N T T E X H N F I A U O R D A I N I
D V I X R D S A M T U N Q H V N B A G S
X V Q R Y J W S X M X X G U E W E X X H
J R N Z S F U Y T O U G I W R D A Q L O
H L O N D T S J Y G E M C G W Q U H U N
Q W I C P D B S L I N R Z X K A T P R E
S A O A Q O X O H U M O R T J E I J Z S
X E H P C M T D R J F T M M S P F E G T
H E S T I A T E M N W O R D E R U D E Y
U I I G E N E S I S A T R B W A L V G G
Q A A Y K O V A R B M C Y F G R U W C N
S E C O N D K B E A A C C U S T O M M O
```

LABAN	COUNTRY	FIRSTBORN	GENESIS
DISHONESTY	HESITATE	CUSTOM	QUOTED
ORDER	SECOND	BEAUTIFUL	EYED
LEAH	EVERYONE	HOLINESS	VAIN
EXPECTATION	COMPENSATE	WEDDING	ORDAIN

Morning

O Lord, thou hast pleaded the causes of my soul;
thou hast redeemed my life.
—Lamentations 3:58

Notice how positively the prophet spoke. He did not say, "I hope, I trust, I sometimes think that God has pleaded the causes of my soul." Instead, he spoke of it as a matter of fact not to be disputed. *"Thou hast pleaded the causes of my soul."* Let us, by the aid of the gracious Comforter, shake off those doubts and fears that so often mar our peace and comfort. May this be our prayer: that we may be done with the harsh, croaking voice of surmise and suspicion and be able to speak with the clear, melodious voice of full assurance. Notice how gratefully the prophet spoke, ascribing all the glory to God alone! There was not a word concerning himself or his own pleadings. He did not ascribe his deliverance in any measure to any man, much less to his own merit; but he said, *"Thou"*—*"O Lord, thou hast pleaded the causes of my soul; thou hast redeemed my life."* A grateful spirit should be cultivated by the Christian; especially after deliverances we should prepare a song for our God. Earth should be a temple filled with the songs of grateful saints, and every day should be a smoking censor, filled with the sweet incense of thanksgiving. How joyful Jeremiah seemed to be while he recorded the Lord's mercy! How triumphantly he lifted up the strain! He had been in the low dungeon, and even now, he is considered to be the weeping prophet; yet in the very book that is called Lamentations, clear as the song of Miriam when she dashed her fingers against the tabor, shrill as the note of Deborah when she met Barak with shouts of victory, we hear the voice of Jeremiah going up to heaven—*"Thou hast pleaded the causes of my soul; thou hast redeemed my life."* Children of God, seek after a vital experience of the Lord's lovingkindness. When you have it, speak positively of it, sing gratefully, and shout triumphantly.

```
V K P D A N X M G A J F L C Z W N I T C
U W J O M K Z Q I J L D A U G H H U H R
O G E L S K P U M F V B M L J A A G A U
G Q R B G I E T T D H H E T H H R J N S
G F S A N D T G A N F U N I P L S Q K U
P D C R B W U I O B C Q T V F U H P S S
J G A A V F V N V Y O I A A E O H W G P
P J V K R N L Q G E M R T T D B J I I I
R Q Q Z K X O C W E L Z I E J C P C V C
E C E N S O R S R S O Y O D U D E B I I
A C G O X U H O H O E N N J L B B D N O
D A S C R I B E S R A J S E D S V L G N
M E L O D I O U S U I K D A S H E D Y K
I E L S K P D V Y R R L I E Y D X C I W
U C Z D H E R Z P K A M L N Y T B J U N
Y V R S O A R J D V S T I X G I N B K P
S Q C P A B K J H M Q O T S Z W Y U E T
O F G G P S O E H D D A H H E J V O T E
Q U T W I A U Z R A A N C N O T I C E B
D E B O R A H G V G B M I R I A M U H W
```

LAMENTATIONS	NOTICE	POSITIVELY	SHAKE
HARSH	CROAKING	SURMISE	SUSPICION
MELODIOUS	ASCRIBE	CULTIVATED	CENSOR
THANKSGIVING	DUNGEON	MIRIAM	DASHED
TABOR	SHRILL	DEBORAH	BARAK

Evening

*The conies are but a feeble folk, yet make they
their houses in the rocks.*
—Proverbs 30:26

Conscious of their own natural defenselessness, the coneys resort to burrows in the rocks, and are secure from their enemies. My heart, be willing to glean a lesson from these "*feeble folk.*" You are as weak and as exposed to peril as the timid coney. Therefore, be as wise to seek a shelter. My best security is within the fortifications of an unchangeable Jehovah, where His unalterable promises stand like giant walls of rock. It will be well with you if you can always hide in the bulwarks of His glorious attributes, all of which are guarantees of safety for those who put their trust in Him. May the name of the Lord be blessed, for I have done so, and have found myself like David in Adullam (see 1 Samuel 22:1)—safe from the cruelty of my enemy. I do not now have to discover the blessedness of the man who puts his trust in the Lord. For, long ago, when Satan and my sins pursued me, I fled to the cleft of the Rock Christ Jesus, and in His torn side I found a delightful resting place. My heart, run to Him anew tonight, no matter what your present grief may be. Jesus feels for you; Jesus comforts you; Jesus will help you. No monarch in his impenetrable fortress is more secure than the coney in his rocky burrow. The captain of ten thousand chariots is not one bit better protected than the little dweller in the cleft of the mountain. In Jesus, the weak are strong, and the defenseless are safe. They could not be stronger if they were giants, or safer if they were in heaven. Faith gives to men on earth the protection of the God of heaven. They could not wish for anything more. The coneys cannot build a castle, but they avail themselves of what is already there. Similarly, I cannot make myself a refuge, but Jesus has provided it, His Father has given it, and His Spirit has revealed it. I enter it again tonight and am safe from every foe.

```
P C J Z D F W R Q P P R E F U G E Z Q W
E X S T O V E F C N E N F V F F U R K Q
R Q E B T Y T G B M D S J G G Q W W N C
I M P E N E T R A B L E J W V I U W E O
L U D L Q O H S E C U R I T Y L P R T N
F W P J D F Z B U R R O W S X D M E O E
P P F R T P O O J J C L E F T Y N S Y Y
O K Q E E W F R V V Y O W J F Z D O M S
K E Z O E Z Y S M T Y K F M I B D R O R
F X P V M B F O M A A D U L L A M T N M
B P F N D Y L T T G V X D R Q H I Y A L
W O U W F Z T E K S A H Z F J R P Q R P
G S A D E F E N S E L E S S N E S S C M
G E I R E V E A L E D H G F N T Q B H F
P D M G N Z C R U E L T Y Z Q Q F V X L
F O R T I F I C A T I O N S I L S Z E Q
Y U F C O N I E S E S X E F Q B M K T L
L O Y S C N F M A H V S U Y W I Z Q O G
C G F U N A L T E R A B L E X K Z G Q F
P R O V E R B S F O R T R E S S T U U I
```

CONIES	PROVERBS	DEFENSELESSNESS	CONEYS
RESORT	BURROWS	FEEBLE	EXPOSED
PERIL	SECURITY	FORTIFICATIONS	UNALTERABLE
ADULLAM	CRUELTY	MONARCH	IMPENETRABLE
FORTRESS	CLEFT	REFUGE	REVEALED

Morning

Thou hast made summer and winter.
—Psalm 74:17

My soul, begin this wintry month with your God. The cold snows and the piercing winds both remind you that He keeps His covenant with day and night, and they tend to assure you that He will also keep that glorious covenant that He has made with you in the person of Christ Jesus. He who is true to His word in the revolutions of the seasons of this poor, sin-polluted world will not prove unfaithful in His dealings with His own well-beloved Son. Winter in the soul is by no means a comfortable season, and if it is on you just now, it will be very painful to you. But there is this comfort: namely, that the Lord makes it. He sends the sharp blasts of adversity to nip the buds of expectation. He scatters the frost like ashes over the once verdant meadows of our joy. He casts forth His ice like morsels freezing the streams of our delight. He does it all. He is the great King of winter, and He rules in the realms of frost; therefore, you cannot complain. Losses, crosses, heaviness, sickness, poverty, and a thousand other ills are of the Lord's sending, and they come to us with wise design. Frost kills deadly insects and limits raging diseases; it breaks up the clods and sweetens the soul. Oh, that such good results would always follow our winters of affliction! How we prize the fire just now! How pleasant is its cheerful glow! Let us prize our Lord in the same manner, who is the constant source of warmth and comfort in every time of trouble. Let us draw near to Him and find joy and peace in believing. Let us wrap ourselves in the warm garments of His promises and go forth to labors that are appropriate to the season. To be like the sluggard who will not plough because of the cold will result in severe consequences, for he will have to beg even in the summer and will have nothing.

```
C J H E F D W W I N T R Y P S P P P Q S F
T B H I J S F F B X O A C T Q X B A Y Q
S L U G G A R D R I P O U T C Q L C X G
Z F R O S T T Z E E D J A T E T V G U O
F P D E A D L Y K X E X F F D S D Y N S
O I J Z A K L W C K X Z H A Q C C T F L
I E F Y P Z A V S E M F I A O A Y S A S
T R S A P O L D U F L V S N E T S Q I N
S C P Y R D I V C Y E V F O G T H C T O
W I P Z O P A S G W F K C R R E L X H W
Y N H R P T H Q E U D I G G W R C Z F S
U G B E R Z X N D I S E A S E S I W U S
I F L I I G V H A P X B X W P R V O L W
B K A O A A U I A Z B C J V A H E R Q I
X H S R T Z Z G I P V U K D I Q R L V F
W A T V E B F U G N M T D I N W D D I V
A P S A Q E M O R S E L S S F M A M N R
M V D Y A A I S P T O O H H U B N G N S
L R E V O L U T I O N S W Q L B T B K H
E B I K A I S U M M E R R E A L M S S C
```

SUMMER	WINTRY	SNOWS	PIERCING
REVOLUTIONS	WORLD	UNFAITHFUL	PAINFUL
BLASTS	BUDS	SCATTERS	FROST
VERDANT	MORSELS	FREEZING	REALMS
DEADLY	DISEASES	APPROPRIATE	SLUGGARD

Evening

Oh that men would praise the Lord for his goodness,
and for his wonderful works to the children of men!
—Psalm 107:8

If we complained less and praised more, we would be happier, and God would be more glorified. Let us daily praise God for common mercies—common as we frequently call them, yet so priceless that, when deprived of them, we are ready to perish. Let us bless God for the eyes with which we behold the sun, for the health and strength to walk around, for the bread we eat, for the clothing we wear. Let us praise Him that we are not cast out among the hopeless or confined among the guilty. Let us thank Him for liberty, for friends, for family, and for comforts. Let us praise Him, in fact, for everything that we receive from His bounteous hand; for we deserve little, yet we are abundantly endowed. But, beloved, the sweetest and the loudest note in our songs of praise should be of redeeming love. God's redeeming acts toward His chosen are forever the favorite themes of their praise. If we know what redemption means, let us not withhold our sonnets of thanksgiving. We have been redeemed from the power of our corruptions, uplifted from the depth of sin in which we were naturally plunged. We have been led to the cross of Christ. Our shackles of guilt have been broken; we are no longer slaves, but children of the living God. We can anticipate the time when we will be presented before the throne without *"spot, or wrinkle, or any such thing"* (Eph. 5:27). Even now by faith we wave the palm branch and wrap ourselves about with the fair linen that is to be our everlasting array. Will we not unceasingly give thanks to the Lord our Redeemer? Child of God, can you be silent? Awake, awake, inheritors of glory, and lead your *"captivity captive"* (Ps. 68:18), as you cry with David, *"Bless the Lord, O my soul: and all that is within me, bless his holy name"* (Ps. 103:1). Let the new month begin with new songs.

```
L B Y S R Q S P H I M X I D H E I R F I
B Z R N R W E N D O W E D P W K N E A C
X O T E P W A F K I W B N I K U H D M K
P Z O C A P T L X G T E E Q R X E C I C
Q N Y O I D R F K E S A A O K S R P L L
U A Q N S J W N S B V H O R W E I S Y F
A Q S F G E A Z H O J A F E T V K J
H L Y I F O B R O S F D R C F P O C D J
R D Q N A R D F O B I S T Y K T R D O L
X H O E W P N G C U S L Z V T L S B C O
F Q O D A J C H L Q N D B H O H E Q D U
X S V P K C L F D F Y D Q N L Y I S B D
M B B P E L W L D E P R I V E D H N G E
P D J Y J L N I M M Z U Q R J N Y C G S
L R S T K C E C O R R U P T I O N S Q T
U Z L U U S J S Y B P K W Y L A M P X F
L F U W P X X W S K N N I G L B L G Y T
S O N N E T S P Z Y V K B P R A I S E V
Z X T B T K L I N E N T Q W N W E F N X
C O M P L A I N E D V M E R C I E S Y Q
```

PRAISE	COMPLAINED	MERCIES	DEPRIVED
WALK	AROUND	BREAD	WEAR
HOPELESS	CONFINED	FAMILY	EVERYTHING
ENDOWED	LOUDEST	SONNETS	CORRUPTIONS
SHACKLES	LINEN	AWAKE	INHERITORS

191

Morning

Orpah kissed her mother in law; but Ruth clave unto her.
—Ruth 1:14

Both Orpah and Ruth had affection for Naomi. That is why they set out with her on her return to the land of Judah. But the hour of testing came. Naomi most unselfishly set before each of them the trials that awaited them. If they cared for ease and comfort, she encouraged them to return to their Moabite friends. At first both of them declared that they would cast in their lot with the Lord's people; but on further consideration, Orpah, with much grief and a respectful kiss, left her mother-in-law and her people and her God. She went back to her idolatrous friends. Ruth, however, with all her heart gave herself up to the God of her mother-in-law. It is one thing to love the ways of the Lord when all is fair, and quite another to cleave to them under all discouragement and difficulties. The kiss of outward profession is very cheap and easy, but the practical cleaving to the Lord, which must show itself in holy decision for truth and holiness, is not so small a matter. How does the case stand with us? Are our hearts fixed on Jesus? Is the sacrifice bound with cords to the horns of the altar? Have we counted the cost, and are we solemnly ready to suffer all worldly loss for the Master's sake? The future gain will be an abundant recompense, for Egypt's treasures are not to be compared with the glory to be revealed. Orpah is heard of no more; in glorious ease and idolatrous pleasure her life melts into the gloom of death. But Ruth lives in history and in heaven, for grace has placed her in the noble line from which came the King of Kings. Blessed among women will those be who for Christ's sake can renounce all; but forgotten and worse than forgotten will those be who in the hour of temptation do violence to conscience and turn back to the world. Oh, that this morning we may not be content with the form of devotion, which may be no better than Orpah's kiss, but may the Holy Spirit work in us a cleaving of our whole hearts to our Lord Jesus.

```
I V O P P P C Q L P B M O A B I T E P E
A U Z O N H Y Q R H D Z K X D R S M R A
J C O N S I D E R A T I O N I E I I A Q
B J I I F U R T H E R Y F M S T H A C E
R K R G M F W E P S X O P C U N U T L
Y Y L H M I C O X N Q B R M O R X K I W
S P R O F E S S I O N E G R U N X A C V
M C Z D F U R X L P F U O X R L W C A P
I Y P M W M O T H E R N T W A Z J X L Z
H P H V A K H M J P R S T X G U M D C A
Z S D E C L A R E D A E E F E H E G H M
D M E W Z R C Q S Q S L N U M M L J E M
L I R T E S T I N G W F P J E X T V A U
U E Q Z G F Z O Q D V I S E N Z S R P K
V J Q J E I Q O U J B S D D T G J H L R
L U V Y X B G K R R Y H E I K M X Q P S
X D I D T E Q W Q P T L P A Z F G Y W A
H A C J M C Z S V L A Y D N A O M I O G
Z H C H I S T O R Y X H J B C L A V E B
U D E C I S I O N P V E Y W R M M P H R
```

ORPAH	MOTHER	CLAVE	NAOMI
RETURN	JUDAH	TESTING	UNSELFISHLY
MOABITE	DECLARED	FURTHER	CONSIDERATION
DISCOURAGEMENT	PROFESSION	CHEAP	PRACTICAL
DECISION	MELTS	HISTORY	FORGOTTEN

Evening

And lay thy foundations with sapphires.
—Isaiah 54:11

Not only that which is seen of the church of God, but also that which is unseen, is fair and precious. Foundations are out of sight. As long as they are firm, it is not expected that they should be valuable. But in Jehovah's work, everything is from Him; nothing is worthless or defective. The deep foundations of the work of grace are as precious sapphires; no human mind is able to measure their glory. We build on the covenant of grace, which is firmer than diamonds and as enduring as jewels on which age spends itself in vain. Sapphire foundations are eternal, and the covenant lasts throughout the lifetime of the Almighty. Another foundation is the person of the Lord Jesus, which is as clear, spotless, everlasting, and beautiful as the sapphire. It blends the deep blue of earth's ever-rolling ocean and the azure of its all-embracing sky. Once, as our Lord stood covered with His own blood, He might have been compared to the ruby; but now we see Him radiant with the soft blue of love, an abundant, everlasting, and deep love. Our eternal hopes are built on the justice and the faithfulness of God, which are as clear and cloudless as the sapphire. We are not saved by a compromise, by mercy defeating justice or law suspending its operations; no, we defy the eagle's eye to detect a flaw in the groundwork of our confidence—our foundation is of sapphire, and it will endure the fire. The Lord Himself has laid the foundation of His people's hopes. It is a matter for grave inquiry whether our hopes are built on such a basis. Good works and ceremonies are not a foundation of sapphires, but of "*wood, hay,* [and] *stubble*" (1 Cor. 3:12); neither are they laid by God, but by our own conceit. Foundations will all be tried before long. Woe unto him whose lofty tower comes down with a crash, because it is based on quicksand. He who is built on sapphires may await storm or fire with calmness, for he will withstand the test.

```
A O K M B C N N W U N Y D R K Y W E P O
S J G C C B E C Z O O R Q P H P L Y U C
U G S X O J K K B L R D Z H P O C P A E
S Z P Z M V U V M S S T D Q J B Y C S R
P D E R P M D E A E T W H E P A W P A E
E P N F R U D E C Q C U D L T C E O P M
N P D L O F M Z F O M W B R E E R H P O
D Y S I M U A X H E E Q S B T S C A H N
I H X B I V S P H Y A B X S L S S T I I
N X R I S V P R T B E T U X K E R H R E
G H J I E M E M B R A C I N G D B T E S
W O L S Q F M T G R C F C N D E U B S D
A L I F E T I M E R U B Y U G F I R D V
W U Q X A I X P M W C B L U E E L N P B
M S K P K Z L J N E R F Y W I C D F F L
O C Z R N A U S P P Z D G X T T E V F E
P V M K F U H R Y W N L Q M Z I F M Z N
F L A W B Z R V E F Y Z V J J V A H F D
V A L U A B L E W R W H F P B E M S T S
L B Y L X R C K N J E W E L S G J E W D
```

SAPPHIRES	VALUABLE	WORTHLESS	DEFECTIVE
BUILD	JEWELS	SPENDS	LIFETIME
BLENDS	BLUE	AZURE	EMBRACING
RUBY	COMPROMISE	DEFEATING	SUSPENDING
DETECT	FLAW	CEREMONIES	STUBBLE

Morning

Rend your heart, and not your garments.
—Joel 2:13

Tearing one's garments and other outward signs of religious emotion are easily manifested and are frequently hypocritical. To feel true repentance is far more difficult; consequently, it is far less common. Men will attend to the most multiplied and minute ceremonial regulations, for such things are pleasing to the flesh. True religion, however, is too humbling, too heart-searching, too thorough for the tastes of carnal men. They prefer something more ostentatious, flimsy, and worldly. Outward observances are temporarily comfortable; eye and ear are pleased, self-conceit is fed, and self-righteousness is puffed up. But they are ultimately misleading, for at the point of death, and on the Judgment Day, the soul needs something more substantial than ceremonies and rituals to lean on. Apart from vital godliness, all religion is utterly vain. Offered without a sincere heart, every form of worship is a solemn sham and an impudent mockery of the majesty of heaven. Heartrending is a divine operation and is solemnly felt. It is a secret grief that is personally experienced, not in mere form, but as a deep, soul-moving work of the Holy Spirit on the inmost heart of each believer. It is not a matter to be merely talked about and believed in, but keenly and sensitively felt in every living child of the living God. It is powerfully humiliating and completely sin-purging; but then, it is sweetly preparative for those gracious consolations that proud spirits are unable to receive. It is distinctly discriminating, for it belongs to the elect of God, and to them alone. The text commands us to rend our hearts, but they are naturally hard as marble. How, then, can this be done? We must take them to Calvary. A dying Savior's voice rent the rocks once, and it is as powerful now. Blessed Spirit, let us hear the death cries of Jesus, and our hearts will be rent even as men tear their clothes in the times of great sorrow.

```
T O Z P U F F E D F A S N C Q C S L T S
Y T R G G S U T N X D C F T W Q I S H B
G X O I B Y T T E A R I N G U X N U O D
M G C R T E M P O R A R I L Y C C B V L
I M A E R U X V Y R R D Z Y V R E S M O
S A L G M I A B O R N C N A V S R T D S
L R V U T F G L C Q L J P V A X E A R T
E B A L A X N H S C L D W K F M K N K E
A L R A Z W E A T M G Y S S P I S T K N
D E Y T D Y R D B E T J N T F C O I W T
I L Y I A Q V E C E O J O E L W L A E A
N X T O F C V C N D G U E G C X H L U T
G B H N Y S O U L D Z J S I A F J I F I
I I V S E Z O J Z L B O E N B B J J L O
B V J U L T I M A T E L Y Y E X P Y I U
Q G M P W I U A J G H U I X V S T H M S
J U H R U I M P U D E N T L W S S N S U
N V G D I S C R I M I N A T I N G I Y C
J X Z U W D H I N G E A S I L Y A Q O E
H Y P O C R I T I C A L J X N B A U D D
```

REND	JOEL	TEARING	EASILY
HYPOCRITICAL	REGULATIONS	OSTENTATIOUS	FLIMSY
TEMPORARILY	RIGHTEOUSNESS	PUFFED	ULTIMATELY
MISLEADING	SUBSTANTIAL	RITUALS	SINCERE
IMPUDENT	DISCRIMINATING	MARBLE	CALVARY

Evening

Be thou diligent to know the state of thy flocks,
and look well to thy herds.
—Proverbs 27:23

Every wise businessman will periodically take stock of his company. He will update his accounts, examine his inventory, and evaluate whether his trade is prospering or declining. Every man who is wise in the kingdom of heaven will cry, *"Search me, O God, and know my heart: try me"* (Ps. 139:23). He will frequently set apart special seasons for self-examination, to discover whether things are right between God and his soul. The God whom we worship is a great heart-searcher. In times past, His servants knew Him as the Lord who searches the heart and examines the minds of His children. (See Jeremiah 17:10.) Let me encourage you in His name to diligently search and solemnly investigate your spiritual condition, lest you come short of the promised rest. That which every wise man does, that which God Himself does with us all, I exhort you to do with yourself this evening. Let the oldest saint look well to the fundamentals of his faith, for gray heads may cover black hearts. Do not let the young believer despise the word of warning, for the greenness of youth may be joined to the rottenness of hypocrisy. Every now and then a cedar falls into our midst. The enemy still continues to sow tares among the wheat. It is not my aim to introduce doubts and fears into your mind; instead, I hope that the rough wind of self-examination may help to drive them away. It is not security, but carnal security, that we want to kill; not confidence, but fleshly confidence, that we want to overthrow; not peace, but false peace, that we want to destroy. By the precious blood of Christ, which was not shed to make you a hypocrite, but so that sincere souls might show forth His praise, I beg you, search and look, lest in the end it will be said of you, "MENE, MENE...TEKEL; *thou art weighed in the balances, and art found wanting"* (Dan. 5:25, 27).

```
M U O K P A C C D E B N N L W N D Z J M
P Z E L E I R U D B F J C R H K G Z P Y
E Q Y U X V M H Y I J Y X K E R R R K F
R K M O A I A D E T F U N U A X A O C M
I X Y N U C N L J R C H Z R T O Y T U Q
O P W N Q T G V U X D T F U P D A T E T
D R Y S H T H Q E A L S C F Q Y S E I R
I N V E N T O R Y S T O C L E Y V N G A
C S Z C H P M F V G T E Z O R O B N W D
A O T M A X V A T G R I D Q R R K E C E
L I H O H H L T C W Z E G L X Q Q S Y H
L R E A C M F Z Z C V D E A T C S S V N
Y Y C M O K O U W B O K E N T G G Z O Q
E X T V T V O A A F W U I U N E T Z Q L
P B O V E R T H R O W M N B G E O V A E
Y A F W C O M P A N Y N I T Z O S P Z A
S P M R P R O S P E R I N G S W U S C L
F G B B J C C H R Z V Z I W R W U S G W
E F U N D A M E N T A L S P T A R E S O
W M C Q K B U S I N E S S M A N F S P Z
```

HERDS	BUSINESSMAN	PERIODICALLY	STOCK
COMPANY	UPDATE	ACCOUNTS	INVENTORY
EVALUATE	TRADE	PROSPERING	INVESTIGATE
FUNDAMENTALS	GRAY	GREENNESS	YOUTH
ROTTENNESS	TARES	WHEAT	OVERTHROW

Morning

Behold, a virgin shall conceive, and bear a son,
and shall call his name Immanuel.
—Isaiah 7:14

Let us go today to Bethlehem, and, in company with wondering shepherds and adoring Magi, let us see Him who was born King of the Jews; for we, by faith, can claim an interest in Him and can sing, *"Unto us a child is born, unto us a son is given"* (Isa. 9:6). Jesus is Jehovah incarnate, our Lord and our God, yet our Brother and Friend. Let us adore and admire Him. Let us notice at the very first glance His miraculous conception. It was a thing unheard of before, and unparalleled since, that a virgin should conceive and bear a son. *"The LORD hath created a new thing in the earth, a woman shall compass a man"* (Jer. 31:22). The first promise involved the seed of the woman—not the offspring of the man. Since adventuresome woman led the way in the sin that brought forth Paradise lost, she, and she alone, ushers in the One who could regain paradise. Our Savior, although truly Man, was, as to His human nature, the Holy One of God. By the power of the Holy Spirit, He was born of the virgin without the taint of original sin, which belongs to all those who are born of the flesh. Let us reverently bow before the holy Child, whose innocence restores to manhood its ancient glory. Let us pray that He may be formed in us, *"the hope of glory"* (Col. 1:27). Do not fail to note His humble parentage. Our morning portion describes His mother as simply *"a virgin,"* not a princess, prophetess, or a matron of a large estate. True, her lineage was not to be despised, for the blood of kings ran in her veins; nor was her mind a weak and untaught one, for she could sing most sweetly a song of praise. Yet how humble her position, how poor the man to whom she stood betrothed, and how miserable the accommodation afforded to the newborn King!…We esteem every day alike, but still, as the seasons and the general custom suggest thoughts of Jesus, let us joyfully remember our dear Redeemer's glorious birth.

```
X M C P D Z W C I N C A R N A T E M V S
N I E O G F C P O N N C D G P Y X A A C
M R P I M P R O O N F P G P X E N N Z J
Y A A Z K T K P N F C S C U O H K H E A
I C F C H X U Q D C F E Q E C J D O M Z
Q U S W X H A T X D E S P B E B S O S F
L L V I R G I N J D T I P T K T U D K O
I O Y T V W N R W I U O V R I G I S H U
N U V W F R H R E G A I N E I O C J K S
E S O I A M J H F P A W X Q R N N P U H
A T B B D Y D B D N E W B O R N G G N E
G Q D A D V E N T U R E S O M E K F H R
E I X I N N O C E N C E T Y G P D N E S
S H S Q P R I N C E S S L Y H W O A A O
A C C O M M O D A T I O N H I U E L R S
P X U R K W K F U T V J S A Z M T E D L
N J B C L I W E U C C C G P E Y A D E H
X V Y C B K Q X J I R C Y G V U F G J V
P A R E N T A G E Q U N T A U G H T I W
T Z P U C B L B E T H L E H E M J G Q G
```

VIRGIN	CONCEIVE	BETHLEHEM	MAGI
INCARNATE	MIRACULOUS	CONCEPTION	UNHEARD
OFFSPRING	ADVENTURESOME	USHERS	REGAIN
INNOCENCE	MANHOOD	PARENTAGE	PRINCESS
LINEAGE	UNTAUGHT	ACCOMMODATION	NEWBORN

Evening

*And it was so, when the days of their feasting were gone about,
that Job sent and sanctified them, and rose up early in the morning,
and offered burnt offerings according to the number of them all.*
—Job 1:5

What the patriarch Job did early in the morning, after the family festivities, would be good for the believer to do for himself before he rests tonight. Amid the cheerfulness of family gatherings, it is easy to slide into sinful frivolities and to forget our avowed character as Christians. It should not be so, but it is. Our days of celebrating are very seldom days of sanctified enjoyment; too frequently, they degenerate into unholy levity. There is a joy that is as pure and sanctifying as though one bathed in the rivers of Eden.

Holy gratitude should be as purifying an element as grief. Unfortunately, for our poor hearts, the fact is that the *"house of mourning"* (Eccl. 7:2) is better than the *"house of feasting"* (v. 2). Come, believer, in what have you sinned today? Have you been forgetful of your high calling? Have you been as those who speak idle words and have loose tongues? Then confess the sin, and fly to the Sacrifice. The Sacrifice sanctifies. The precious blood of the slain Lamb removes the guilt and purges away the defilement of our sins of ignorance and carelessness.

Behold the Lamb of God, which taketh away the sin of the world. (John 1:29)

The best ending for a Christmas Day would be to wash anew in the cleansing fountain. Believer, come to this sacrifice continually; if it is good to do so tonight, it is good every night. To live at the altar is the privilege of the royal priesthood. As great as it is, sin is nevertheless no cause for despair, since believers may yet again draw near to the sin-atoning Sacrifice, and have their consciences purged from dead works.

Gladly I close this festive day, Grasping the altar's hallow'd horn;
My slips and faults are washed away, The Lamb has all my trespass borne.

```
K S O V P V U D T O N I G H T W X N B S
A Y I V E P M R E P J W B S F A X E W M
I L E V I T Y N A G A B A U W E R V F O
M Q E F C B A K O R E I T Y V H N E C L
Q L P X T R A E F K D N H S O P N R E K
L R C O R A D I G S T T E M M I X T L P
S P P E N J O Y M E N T D R U N M H E F
M K U D Q H V R W N A M Y K A U S E B E
S O N S M M R B U R N T C W K T J L R S
R D Q F K B Z T H D R N J S P V E E A T
J E Y P Z L E F E S T I V I T I E S T I
S S H V H G C J W J O N G D G J W S I V
M P X F S E L D O M S T N B B V O Q N E
H A K A V O W E D T Q A L T V N R B G O
M I U W N R O P Q L L A E O Z P G Q L S
C R Q T D C K S P X I F Y W O B I J L L
R C H R I S T M A S K B C C F S Y S H I
O D N D X U K D O G N U W J A O E A P D
D A J R E D E N B B T P B D U U H P I E
R O F K M N K L J T O N G U E S J W D Z
```

JOB	BURNT	SONS	FESTIVITIES
TONIGHT	SLIDE	AVOWED	CELEBRATING
SELDOM	ENJOYMENT	DEGENERATE	LEVITY
BATHED	EDEN	LOOSE	TONGUES
CHRISTMAS	NEVERTHELESS	DESPAIR	FESTIVE

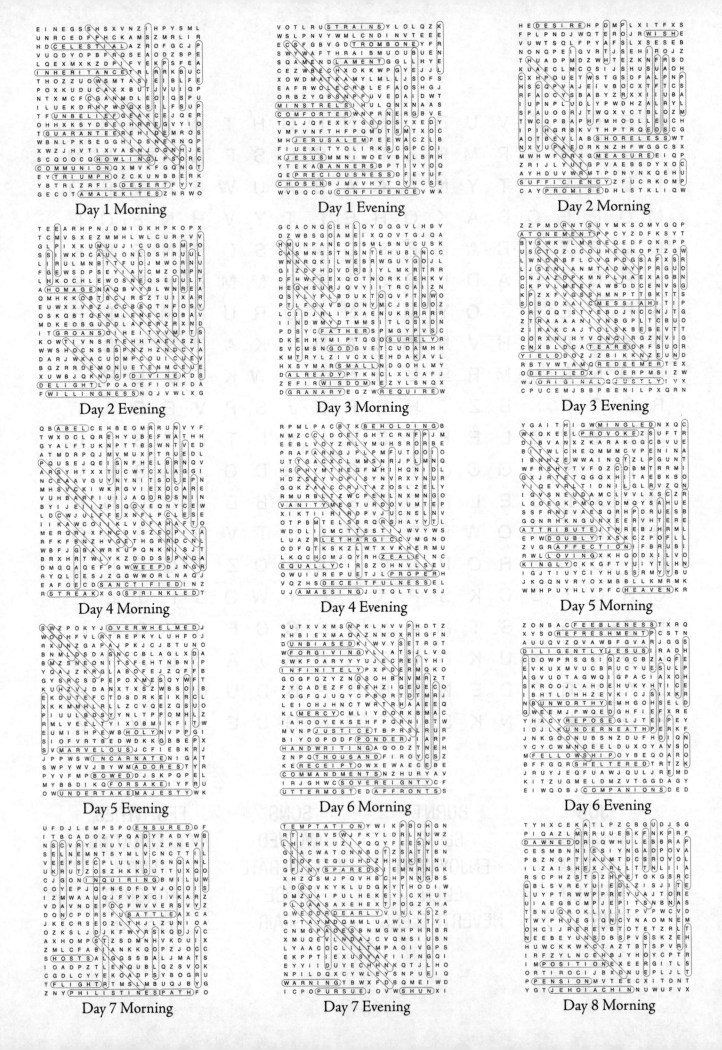

Day 1 Morning

Day 1 Evening

Day 2 Morning

Day 2 Evening

Day 3 Morning

Day 3 Evening

Day 4 Morning

Day 4 Evening

Day 5 Morning

Day 5 Evening

Day 6 Morning

Day 6 Evening

Day 7 Morning

Day 7 Evening

Day 8 Morning

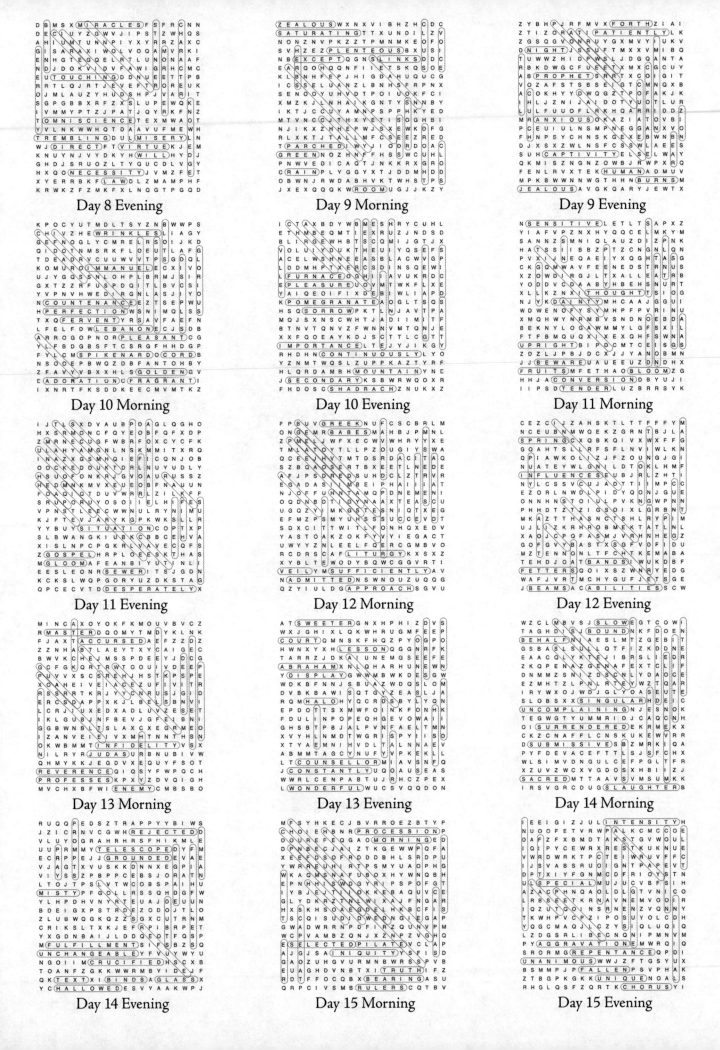

Day 8 Evening

Day 9 Morning

Day 9 Evening

Day 10 Morning

Day 10 Evening

Day 11 Morning

Day 11 Evening

Day 12 Morning

Day 12 Evening

Day 13 Morning

Day 13 Evening

Day 14 Morning

Day 14 Evening

Day 15 Morning

Day 15 Evening

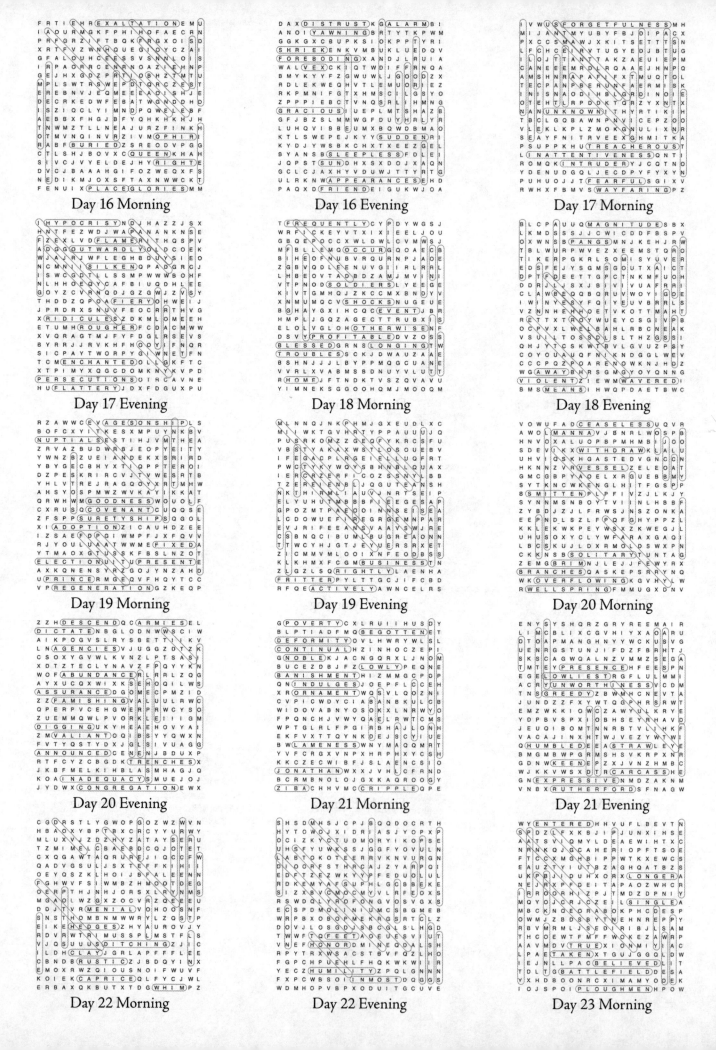

Day 16 Morning

Day 16 Evening

Day 17 Morning

Day 17 Evening

Day 18 Morning

Day 18 Evening

Day 19 Morning

Day 19 Evening

Day 20 Morning

Day 20 Evening

Day 21 Morning

Day 21 Evening

Day 22 Morning

Day 22 Evening

Day 23 Morning

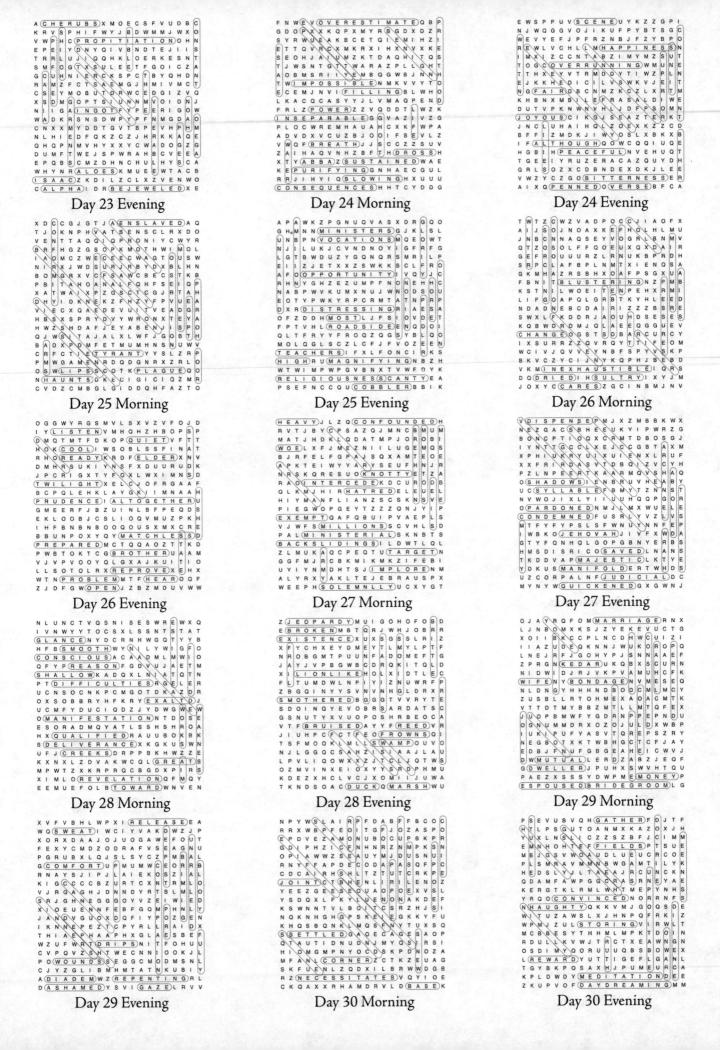

Day 23 Evening

Day 24 Morning

Day 24 Evening

Day 25 Morning

Day 25 Evening

Day 26 Morning

Day 26 Evening

Day 27 Morning

Day 27 Evening

Day 28 Morning

Day 28 Evening

Day 29 Morning

Day 29 Evening

Day 30 Morning

Day 30 Evening

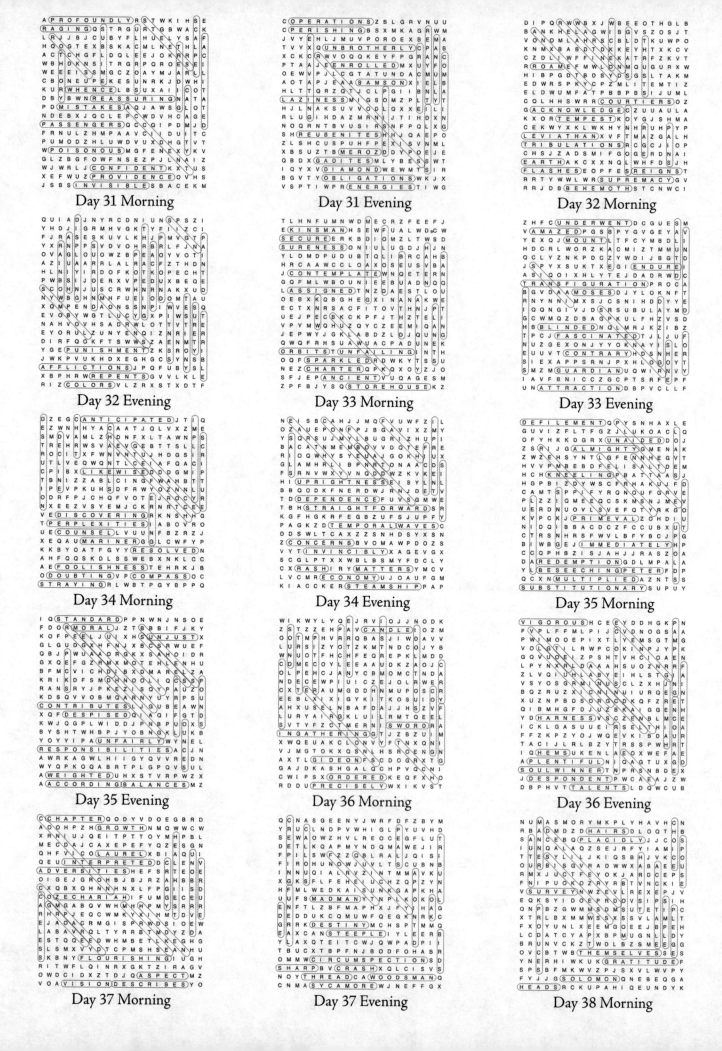

Day 31 Morning

Day 31 Evening

Day 32 Morning

Day 32 Evening

Day 33 Morning

Day 33 Evening

Day 34 Morning

Day 34 Evening

Day 35 Morning

Day 35 Evening

Day 36 Morning

Day 36 Evening

Day 37 Morning

Day 37 Evening

Day 38 Morning

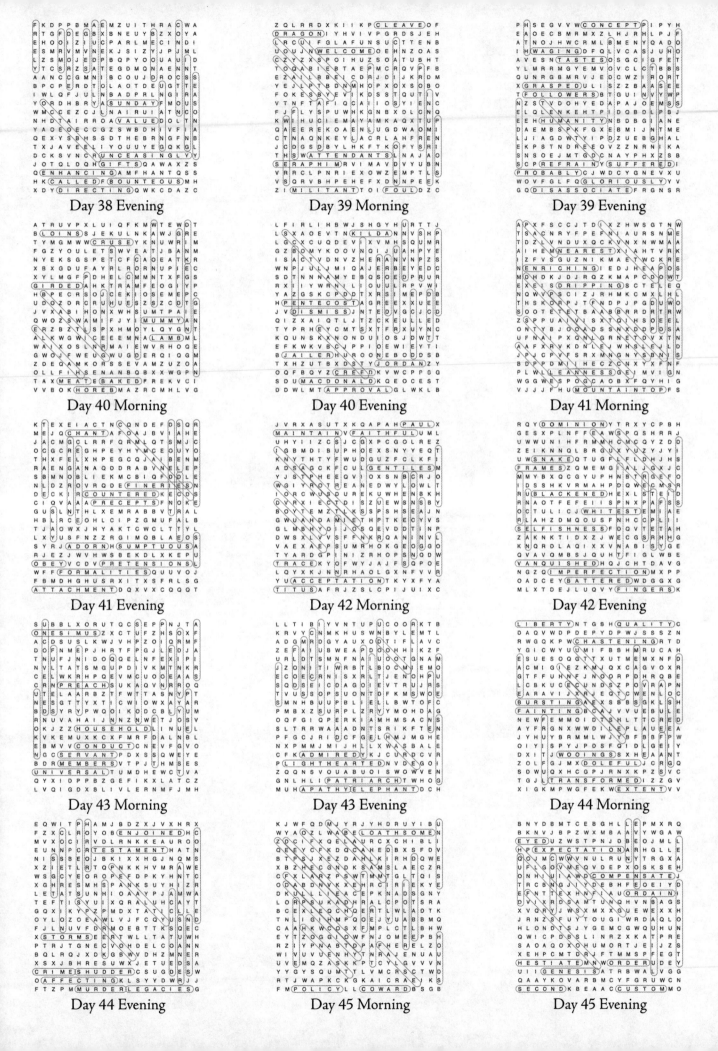

Day 38 Evening

Day 39 Morning

Day 39 Evening

Day 40 Morning

Day 40 Evening

Day 41 Morning

Day 41 Evening

Day 42 Morning

Day 42 Evening

Day 43 Morning

Day 43 Evening

Day 44 Morning

Day 44 Evening

Day 45 Morning

Day 45 Evening

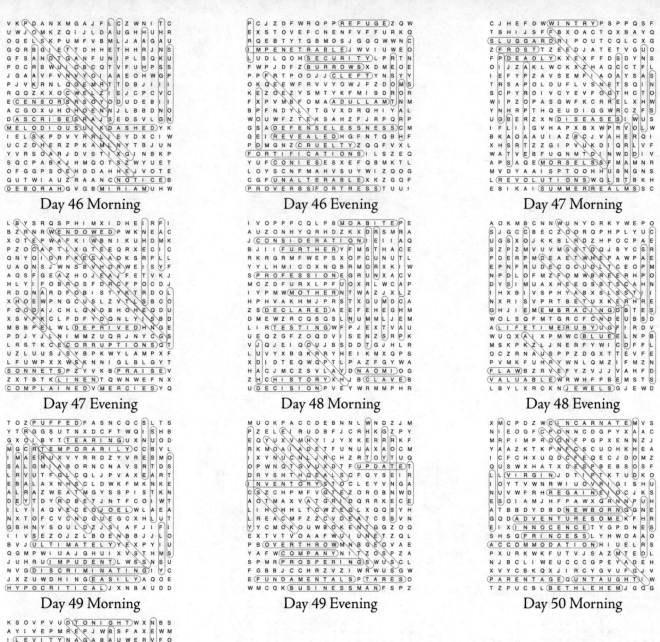

Day 46 Morning

Day 46 Evening

Day 47 Morning

Day 47 Evening

Day 48 Morning

Day 48 Evening

Day 49 Morning

Day 49 Evening

Day 50 Morning

Day 50 Evening